'This is not another quaint book about how outsiders *have* an edge. This is a subversive manual for how outsiders can *carve* an edge for themselves with hard work, creativity and the right mental framework.'

Ryan Holiday, author of *The Obstacle Is the Way*

'This stopped me in my tracks. Robert has articulated and explained something which to many of us is just a feeling of outsider-ness. More than that he has explained what to do about it.'

Richard Newton, bestselling author of
The Little Book of Thinking Big

'Ignore trendy commentators telling you being an outsider's advantageous: it's actually highly disabling. Kelsey gets on top of the issues to find a practical (and uncompromising) way through. With Kelsey's help – being an outsider won't f*** you up.'

Oliver James, author of *They F*** You Up* and *Affluenza*

'*The Outside Edge* is a terrific book for anyone who ever felt they didn't belong. The author has written a highly personal analysis of how outsiders can succeed in work and in life. He has drawn upon a vast range of references across psychology, self-help, literature, philosophy and business to provide advice and encouragement to readers who feel they are not a member of the club. Kelsey has found fulfilment in middle age by building his own company and becoming a husband and father, and describes his journey – trying to be cool but feeling constantly alienated – brilliantly. I found *The Outside Edge* to be both pragmatic and uplifting. If you are looking for an enjoyable guide to both meaning and purpose in the 21st century, then I strongly recommend this title.'

Luke Johnson, *The Sunday Times* columnist,
author of *Start It Up* and Chairman of the Centre for Entrepreneurs

'This is a thorough investigation into a neglected and often misunderstood area. Empathising with outsiders isn't always easy – they are the (often self-declared) 'misfits' after all. And, as Kelsey points out, outsiders themselves are prone to 'distorted empathy' (i.e. identifying with the bad guy). Yet this makes Kelsey's highly readable text and positive methodology all the more noteworthy.'

Roman Krznaric, author of *Empathy: Why it Matters,
and How to Get it,* and *The Wonderbox:
Curious Histories of How to Live*

'Robert's book is a brilliant resource for anyone who feels stuck in the 'grey zone' or is working in the area of people development. It helps to explain why people behave in the way that they do, and provides many practical ideas and tips to help them and/or others make the changes they need to find meaning and purpose.'

Lindsey Agness, founder and managing director of The Change Corporation
and author of *Change Your Life with NLP*

'This is a book that totally resonates. Outsiders tend not to be positive thinkers and pessimists can find themselves feeling shut out. Kelsey not only understands this, but finds a way through. *The Outside Edge* is defensive pessimism in action. Bravo!'

Julie K. Norem PhD, author of
The Positive Power of Negative Thinking

'This is an excellent read packed with both cautionary tales and optimistic insight, for anyone who's ever felt on the periphery. It's revealing, compelling and highly practical – not least in offering life-skills to those without the innate advantages of the insider.'

Helena Pozniak, life-skills writer for the
Daily Telegraph, The Guardian, The Independent and elsewhere

'As Kelsey so eloquently demonstrates, outsiders are often highly creative, and are usually best placed pursuing entrepreneurial ambitions – something that certainly chimes with my own outlook. What's unique about this book, however, is Kelsey's explanation of the sometimes discomforting reasons why people become estranged from their tribe. Its message is uncompromisingly positive, although it also deals well with the genuine struggles outsiders face.'

Michael Jacobsen, serial entrepreneur and author of
The Business of Creativity

'I can't believe how many excellent insights Kelsey has drawn from such diverse and wise sources. With his characteristic honesty and ability to reflect on personal experience, he has created an inspiring and practical guide for outsiders. Kelsey's books have the rare quality of encouraging the reader to reach beyond current limitations without over-promising, denying our vulnerability, or pretending that life isn't sometimes (often) unpredictable, random, and difficult. *The Outside Edge* is a book outsiders will certainly appreciate if we want to increase our chances of success and well-being, however we define them, in a world made, and dominated, by insiders.'

Ian Aspin, author of *How to Be a Super Human:
Using the Amazing Power of Social Networks*

'Having helped generate 60 start-ups in six years, I've seen many outsiders succeed – on their own terms – as entrepreneurs. To make the most of their unique perspective, however, outsiders *must* acquire a degree of self-awareness as well as certain specific skills: knowledge that's expressed brilliantly in this book, which I heartily recommend.'

Martin Bjergegaard, co-founder of Rainmaking
and Startupbootcamp and best-selling author
of *Winning without Losing*

The Outside *Edge*

How Outsiders Can Succeed in a World Made By Insiders

Robert Kelsey

CAPSTONE
A Wiley Brand

This edition first published 2015
© 2015 What's Stopping You Ltd
What's Stopping You? is a trademark of What's Stopping You Ltd?

Registered office

John Wiley and Sons Ltd, The Atrium, Southern Gate, Chichester, West Sussex, PO19 8SQ, United Kingdom

For details of our global editorial offices, for customer services and for information about how to apply for permission to reuse the copyright material in this book please see our website at www.wiley.com.

Library of Congress Cataloging-in-Publication Data
Kelsey, Robert
  The outside edge : how outsiders can succeed in a world made by insiders / Robert Kelsey.
     pages cm
  Includes bibliographical references and index.
  ISBN 978-0-857-08575-7 (paperback)
  1. Self-esteem. 2.   Identity (Psychology) 3.   Creative ability.   I. Title.
  BF697.5.S46K455 2015
  158.1—dc23   2014047585
A catalogue record for this book is available from the British Library.

ISBN 978-0-857-08575-7 (paperback) ISBN 978-0-857-08573-3 (ebk)
ISBN 978-0-857-08574-0 (ebk)

Cover design: Wiley
Cover image: ©Rawpixel/shutterstock

Set in 10.13.5pt Sabon LT Std by Thomson Press
Printed in Great Britain by TJ International Ltd, Padstow, Cornwall, UK

To Lucy, George and Eddie

CONTENTS

Contents

INTRODUCTION

DEBUNKING THE OUTSIDER MYTH

'If you really want to hear about it, the first thing you'll probably want to know is where I was born, and what my lousy childhood was like, and how my parents were occupied and all before they had me, and all that David Copperfield kind of crap, but I don't feel like going into it, if you really want to know the truth.'

Holden Caulfield's sleep-deprived meanderings around 1940s New York provide the narrative for probably the most enduring treatise to adolescent alienation ever written. J.D. Salinger's *The Catcher in the Rye* (1951) is an exploration of the contradictions, shallowness and fakery of adult life – as seen through the eyes of a 16-year-old outsider. According to Caulfield, everyone he encounters is a 'phony' – pursuing thinly-disguised self-interest via artificial conventions and a veneer of amiability. It's a world he despises for its hypocrisy and materialistic insincerity. Seeking depth and purity, Cauflield clings to uncorrupted icons such as his kid sister or the ducks in Central Park.

It's a private and lonely rebellion: insightful yet naïve, sensitive yet hateful, individualistic yet aching to be understood. Defiant and insolent despite his inner confusion, Caulfield's inarticulate musings express both the hopes and despair of youth so authentically they've made Salinger's anti-hero the torchbearer for generations of tortured souls, me included. Like millions before and since, I identified with

Caulfield's mix of cynicism and angst – even mimicking his train journey into Manhattan through adolescent forays down the Essex commuter line into London's Liverpool Street Station.

Clutching a day-return ticket, I'd wander the backstreets of the East End: collar up, cigarette in mouth, hands in pocket – the sheer misery of the streets around Petticoat Lane and Spitalfields markets (then, when shut, full of rubbish and winos) reflecting my lonely discomfort at the straightened adulthood I saw ahead of me.

Oh, how I loved Salinger for giving voice to my lonely disaffection.

Salinger's false promise

Yet there's a problem with this vision. While Manhattan and central London are obvious comparatives – and Caulfield and I suffered the same mix or angst and alienation – we had little in common. Unbeknown to me, Caulfield had an *edge*. He was being thrown out of Pencey Prep, an exclusive private school that had equipped him well despite his inability to complete a history paper or enjoy the college football games.

The tutors knew him and even cared for his welfare, and he was captain of the school fencing team. Meanwhile, I was one more mass-produced nobody from a 'bog standard' state education system that expected, and planned for, low attainment. No one looked out for me and I was captain of nothing. So while Caulfield's alienation came from his fear and rejection of the expectations driven by his expensive education, mine came from an altogether different source: exclusion.

In fact, Caulfield was no outsider. He was an insider with attitude. It's a crucial divide, and one giving him an *edge* over the likes of me, who was simply on the edge: as denoted by our behaviour once in the big city. Caulfield confidently bluffed his way into expensive Midtown hotels – blagging alcoholic drinks and dancing with 30-something female tourists – while I kicked around closed markets, maybe engaging a homeless bum in a doorway or nursing a mug of tea in an East End 'caff'.

Of course, *The Catcher in the Rye* is fiction, although Salinger's early adulthood somewhat mirrors that of Caulfield, with the added guilt of benefiting from self-made immigrant parents. Yet this theme of the romantic outsider being – in reality – an elite rejectionist, and therefore someone with an *edge* over less advantaged outsiders, is repeated time and again. A British literary hero of the rebellious classes is George Orwell (1903–50), a man disavowing imperial conformity to chronicle the poor and downtrodden of the interwar years. As social commentary Orwell's writing is explosive – not least his ability to experience the life of an alienated down-and-out or itinerant salesman.

And, like Salinger, Orwell's work has survived through decades of change by tapping into social exclusion via his own alienation. An alienation, what's more, that ran deep enough to reject the affected-revolutionary rhetoric of his fellow bohemians. Indeed, Orwell is a hero of intellectual heretics from both ends of the political spectrum – surely the mark of a true outsider?

Except that Orwell was no outsider. An Old Etonian – and part of the imperial governing class – Orwell, like Caulfield, had an *edge* over his fellow rejectionists. And he also had the indulgence of choice. Tired of roughing it, Orwell would return to his parents' seaside residence in the smart Suffolk resort of Southwold. Here, he could eat well, pursue love interests and perhaps be fitted for a new suit – all while damning the bourgeoisie for their selfish mores, petty snobberies and hypocritical values.

America's outsider here is Ernest Hemingway (1899–1961). A rugged and individualistic 'man's man', Hemingway repudiated societal boundaries by seeking novelty through adventure. His writing is legendary although, again, Hemingway was no outsider. He was the well-educated son of a doctor and musician. And those masculine survivor skills were learnt from his father at the family's second home in rural Michigan: a weekend retreat away from the smart gatherings of upper middle-class suburban Chicago.

As with Orwell, Hemingway pursued extreme individualism out of choice. Again, his expensively-honed skills and family connections gave him the *edge* required for him to profitably pursue macho dreams that indulged his love of European sophistication, hardcore naturalism and the adrenalin of war.

Gladwell's myth exposed

As outsiders, Orwell and Hemingway make poor role models. They renounced conventional attitudes not despite their privileges but because of them – relying on the *edge* their advantages gave them in order to succeed as outsiders. Meanwhile, anybody forsaking such norms without such an *edge* will find such individualism a far harder slog. In fact, they'll likely find it impossible.

Of course, to the observer, such rejection looks and acts outwardly the same. Orwell the tramp looks much like the next guy sleeping under Waterloo Bridge. Yet they couldn't be further apart. Given Orwell's privileges, he had an incentive to sleep rough – not so the outcast beside him, for whom a good Suffolk breakfast, a fitting at Denny's and a mild disagreement with one's publisher are the pursuits of someone from another planet.

Such is the gap between the advantaged and the disadvantaged outsider – such is the *edge* some have and others lack. Not that you'd know it from reading Malcolm Gladwell. In his book – *David and Goliath: Underdogs, Misfits and the Art of Battling Giants* (2013) – that modern-day sage explores the art of success for those without the advantages of the insider. And as the book's title suggests, Gladwell uses that famous biblical battle as his exemplar.

History perceives the underdog to be the shepherd-boy misfit David. Yet, according to Gladwell, David possessed hidden advantages over the warrior-giant Goliath due to his ability to generate new solutions by breaking the rules. Goliath prepared for a straight fight based on his traditional assumptions and military knowledge, and expected to win based on his size. Meanwhile, the outsider David – by refusing armour – ignored convention: instead employing his shepherd's slingshot to fell the colossus.

Life's full of such examples, opines Gladwell – proving that the disadvantaged or excluded can break convention simply by turning it on its head. Dyslexics succeed due to their highly-developed listening skills, he says, while those educated in larger class sizes – something most educationalists think detrimental – benefit from shared learning and collaboration. From the American Revolution to Vietnam, from the Civil Rights movement to Northern Ireland, Gladwell finds history littered with underdogs that were expected to lose due to their disadvantages, yet who overcame obstacles through guile, guts and creativity. Most often – like David and his agile slingshooting – they won because their perceived disadvantages were in fact advantages, giving them an *edge* over their rivals.

Great news. If only it were true.

Unfortunately, it's a myth: the outsider myth – a modern day fallacy that says, to succeed, you have to go against the tide. Be different. In reality, however, it's an option open only to a well-educated elite pursuing their expensively-acquired advantages over the rest of us. Of course, underdogs *can* succeed, just as outsiders *can* change the world. Yet any 'misfit' thinking success is assured simply because they're 'not like other people' is likely to find themselves on the wrong side of history. From 5,000 years of records, Gladwell picks the winners while ignoring the countless occasions outsiders were crushed and forgotten by those utilizing their inherent advantages – their *edge* – over the rest of us.

For Gladwell, disadvantages – such as low educational attainment and social exclusion – are not disadvantages at all. They encourage cooperation, flair and imagination. Yet I think this a cruel trick to play on the millions of people feeling alienated from conventional pursuits while lacking the gilded opportunities of an Orwell or Hemingway, or even a Caulfield. Society's changed since Salinger wrote of Caulfield's bleary-eyed New York wanderings, and even since I kicked around the East End. But it hasn't changed enough to accommodate all those encouraged to think their outsider angst and misfit rage a sure sign their 'gift' is bankable.

The soundtrack of working-class rebellion

Not so, shout the optimists. The world's full of disadvantaged outsiders that made it due to their unique outlook. Take rock 'n' roll. Isn't that the soundtrack to working class rebellion going right back to white kids playing black rhythms to shock their parents in 1950s America? On this side of the pond, pop-music (at least until the 1990s) was virtually defined by alienation: not least in the spawning of multiple musical tribes such as punks, mods, casuals, rude boys or new romantics. Surely, each of these cultural insurgencies contained significant elements of working class rebellion, didn't they? And their revolutionary leaders – whether Ozzy Osbourne, Paul Weller, Johnny Rotten, Terry Hall or Steve Strange – were all authentic working class heroes, weren't they?

Indeed they were. Yet look closely and those preaching anarchy were just as often recoiling from middle-class expectations – from 'making plans for Nigel' – than the limits of working-class aspiration. Sure, the odd back-street band won a deal from the moneymen – producing dancehall fodder for the masses. But nearly all those 1970s superbands – the likes of *Genesis, Pink Floyd, Queen, Fleetwood Mac*, and even *The Clash* – can trace their heritage back to Britain's fee-paying 'public' schools, again proving that rebellion is facilitated by, not despite, the advantages of privilege.

A peculiarly-British twist? Not at all. While researching this book news came of Lou Reed's death. A sad loss, not least because, along with his band (*The Velvet Underground*), he was emblematic of the rebellion pop-music engendered for so many. Reed was billed as an outsider – a label confirmed by his obituaries: *The New York Times* even running the headline 'Outsider Whose Dark Lyrical Vision Helped Shape Rock 'n' Roll'.

Yet Lou Reed's rejection of society owes more to his advantages than any sense of working class rebellion. The son of an accountant, Reed – as the child of successful New York Jewry – led a rather similar, well-educated, adolescence to Salinger. In other words, he was an idiosyncratic member of an elitist club. And this made Reed's rebellion towards the drug-addled dens of New York's underworld a choice, although his sense of rejection was compounded by his parent's ham-fisted efforts to 'cure' his bisexual 'urges'.

In fact, just about everywhere you look for rebellion you find highly-educated people with expensively-honed talents pursuing 'exclusion' as a means of self-expression – something true of music, the arts and literature. And it's even true in business. After all, revolutionary techies Bill Gates (of Microsoft) and Mark Zuckerberg (of Facebook) had wealthy parents and a good college education – seemingly necessary requisites for breaking the mould via entrepreneurial success. Even Richard Branson, the UK's best-known entrepreneurial rebel – and one of the moneymen supporting British pop – is the privately-educated son of a barrister.

Can disadvantaged outsiders prosper?

Stop me if I'm ranting, because the message here isn't one of class envy or 'chippiness'. At least not deliberately. My concern is for the outsider and the fact there's a gulf – despite appearances – between the tools available, and therefore the outcomes, for advantaged against disadvantaged outsiders: for those with or without the *edge* of privilege.

Yet the central premise of this book is not the bemoaning of this reality. It's to establish how disadvantaged outsiders can develop that *edge*. While disagreeing with Gladwell's claim that our disadvantages and/or alienation can work in our favour, my aim here is to help make that very prospect a reality: to give genuine outsiders (not just eccentric elitists) the *edge* required to help them succeed.

Indeed, for every Salinger there's a D.H. Lawrence or Alan Sillitoe: both born to semi-literate Nottinghamshire fathers – one a miner, the other a bicycle factory worker. Yet both became era-defining writers. In fact, Sillitoe's *The Loneliness of the Long Distance Runner* (1959) stands alongside *The Catcher in the Rye* as a treatise to, this time working class, alienation and rebellion.

7

For every Lou Reed there's a David Bowie (the Brixton-born son of a waitress and charity worker); or Andy Warhol (Reed's mentor and patron, and the son of an immigrant Pennsylvanian miner); or Tracey Emin (a teenage rape victim from the wrong part of Kent with cross-Romany/Turk-Cypriot parentage).

And for every Richard Branson there's Apple's Steve Jobs (the adopted son of a garage mechanic); or omni-inventor Thomas Edison (the near-deaf youngest child of a political refugee); or Starbucks' Howard Schultz (the son of a Brooklyn truck driver).

Yet don't be fooled. The Edisons and the Emins – as well as the Bowies and Warhols – are far from the norm. Insiders are the norm. It's their world, with advantaged outsiders no more than insiders with an attitude – though still utilizing the *edge* gained from their inherent advantages in pursuit of their (usually creative) self-expression. Disadvantaged outsiders have to make it *despite* their sometimes highly-disabling attributes, not because of them. Gladwell's wrong on this one, though that's where this book comes in.

Making rebellion count

Being a disadvantaged outsider is usually a one-way ticket to economic and social exclusion: a message as true of race, gender, age and sexuality as it is for class. Forget the noise that anything's possible – rebellion's end for those without the *edge* of inherited or acquired privilege (in whatever form) more usually involves confusion, isolation, failure and surrender. More outsiders commit suicide than conquer the world using their original perspective: a depressing conclusion that every word in this book is aimed at preventing.

If we're to avoid such a fate, we must forge an *edge* for ourselves: one that helps us cut through the discrimination and barriers we face (both seen and unseen). As stated, those that feel alienated – not by their guilty advantages but due to the lack of them – *can* break conventions. And this can, if successful, lead to revolutionary change. Many advances in all human fields have been brought about by those 'thinking outside the box' – most often due to their exclusion from those 'inside the box'. We look at the world as if watching a play unfold, allowing us to observe and understand it in ways not available to the players themselves.

This is a unique vantage point. It's also one offering genuine outsiders an even sharper *edge* than all those eccentric insiders utilizing their inherent social booty: as long as we can calculate a singular direction and hone the skills required to progress. If we can develop that unique perspective and – importantly – find a way of getting others to listen, then rebellion's end could well bring about revolutionary change. And that sure beats kicking around the East End with the weight of the world on your shoulders.

Despite the myth peddled by Gladwell (and others), the attributes of genuine outsiders are usually highly disabling – with most successful outsiders no more than insiders with an attitude. Yet that shouldn't prevent us from developing an advantageous edge. To do so, however, we must first understand how we came to feel so estranged: our task for Part One.

PART ONE
The Making of an Outsider

1

THE MISFITS

First let's recognize the outsider. We're all born to a tribe, and of a landscape. It's inescapable. But we don't all fit in. Some of us – for reasons we'll explore later – become alienated from the others. We're the misfits: rejecting or rejected by the colony. Over time, we develop an outlook that emphasizes the disconnect we feel with our peers. And, soon enough, we're on the edge, looking in – or just as often looking away.

There's nothing inherently enabling about this situation, no matter what the view of fashionable commentators. There are no advantages. There's no *edge* to being on the edge. In fact, over millennia it's a predicament costing misfits dear. Ostracism, bullying, assault – even rape and murder – are the usual results; as is anxiety, loneliness, depression and even suicide for those not a central part of the clan. When the food runs out or the gods need pacifying, it's the outsider that's sacrificed. Hence the anxiety.

Children and animals instinctively know this, and spend their lives jockeying for position. They're vying for centrality, and detest any imposition that hinders the quest. As a child, I rejected school lifts from my father because he drove a Rover 3800 – preferring instead to trudge miles across muddy fields and spend the day with my flares rimmed with the Essex mud that denoted my membership of the clan.

Yet the terror of rejection follows us into adulthood. Even our love of fashion is little more than tribal signalling that we're in with the in-crowd: central rather than peripheral. It says that we're keen to follow our tribal leaders and be part of their 'set' (with flamboyant clothes little more than a bid for leadership). Fortunes are made on the assumption we'll cough up to be on the right side of the velvet rope – touching the nucleus. Nick Jones founded *Soho House* in London on that very premise, with his East London outpost – *Shoreditch House* – a constant reminder of my own inability to integrate with this human core. To forever be the man at street level, peering through frosted glass at a world out of reach.

So where are the advantages? How can rejection and isolation offer anyone an *edge* over their brethren? The truth is they cannot, at least not on their own. Left to its own trajectory, being an outsider involves frustration, anger, rage and – ultimately – surrender. It's totally disabling, especially when the disadvantages are hidden. Claim race, gender, disability or sexuality as encumbrances to your advance, and western society's high-liberalism throws you the law's protection and the media's adulation (though the barriers remain). Claim it's something more personal – your position in the family hierarchy, say, or your sensitivity compared to your peers, or even your poor education – and you're, quite literally, alone: condemned as pathetic and ostracized all the more.

Gaining an *edge* here is much harder, and lonelier, work.

The lost tribe

My claim's certainly pathetic, though it starts with a very modern phenomenon: dislocation. Like everyone, I came from a tribe. And I'm of a landscape. Yet the two didn't marry. We were townies marooned in the countryside. Part of the post-war East London Diaspora, my childhood outlook over a flat Essex mudscape tweaked not the slightest curiosity about the land's use or ownership. It's what writer and 'psycho-geographer' Iain Sinclair labels Empty Quarter Essex – 'a floating landscape . . . there to be seen from passing cars, not to be experienced at first hand,' he writes in *London Orbital* (2002). 'Essex is better remembered than known.'

And I knew it in the 1970s – long before Essex Man became the ambassadors for the 'white trash with cash' tribe that came to dominate millennial tastes in the UK. Then, we were a lost tribe: uprooted from our urban homelands and deposited on the arable steppes beyond Abercrombie's greenbelt.

The indigenous gentry – in their flat caps and Range Rovers – viewed us disdainfully, though we'd return the contempt by vandalizing their tractors or damming their irrigation ditches. Yet we were also despised by the genuinely-poor rural natives. The offspring of farmhands and pea-pickers, they lived in shambolic enclaves with overgrown gardens and barking Rottweilers. That said, their untended plots were integral to the surrounding countryside – as were they – while our presence in the raw, jagged, sapling-dappled housing estates jarred.

Of course, colonists facing hostile natives should tighten as a group. Yet I was an outsider even within my displaced 'white flight' colony. My peers – all tribal warriors in the making – were no more like me than the kids we called 'Garys' from the ragged end of the village. I wanted to integrate but couldn't. Again, this was partly geographic. My cul-de-sac was on a different side of the 'village' from the neat housing estates of my clan. They played happily together – in and out of each other's gardens and bedrooms (as were their parents) – while I languished a million miles (in fact around half-a-mile) from the action.

Even when old enough to join them 'after tea' it meant interrupting well-established group dynamics, which made hard work of integration. So I'd suggest the riskier pursuits. Those vandalism episodes were my idea, as were the 'scrumping' trips to commercial orchards, the smoking parties in the churchyard, the cheeking of passing adults and the winter evenings spent 'garden-hopping' (a fantastically exciting sport involving stealthily traversing rows of back gardens).

Such exploits brought me to the attention of local authorities – including the churchwardens and the old lady running the Post Office. And, before long, I was the troublesome child being discussed through pursed lips and sharp looks. Banned from their houses, the distance between me and my brethren soon became more than geographic: it was sanctioned.

Divorced from our surroundings

Pathetic, indeed – especially for such feelings to last into middle age. But that's how it is for many outsiders. Tiny discomforts, denoting small disconnections that build into a disorientating estrangement. Certainly, bigger issues also count. Latent feelings of homosexuality, for instance, or learning difficulties or even 'genius': all can foster notions of being 'other'. But they're somehow legitimized – not least because clans exist that can accommodate them. Meanwhile, the narrow degrees of separation from clan life are viewed as invalid, a response that only serves to exacerbate the unease – pushing us further towards the edge and making us feel locked inside our own circumstances.

Of course, many declare themselves outsiders, perhaps because it suits their self-image of rugged individualism (as with Hemingway) or creative non-conformity (as with Orwell). And we can hide our discomfort with defiance – even arrogance. Yet, far from being an enabling disposition (one giving us the advantages Gladwell *et al* would have us believe), outsiders tend to exhibit troubling and often highly-disabling attributes that both separate us from the group and, over time, reinforce our exclusion.

Are you an outsider?

So are you an outsider? Chances are it's a question requiring no answer: most people know. Nonetheless, it's worth pointing out what sets us apart, even if it's for cathartic – rather than identification – purposes. And, please note, while there are positives to being an outsider (hence the book), nothing in the traits below offers genuine, disadvantaged, outsiders an *edge*. Quite the opposite.

Sensitivity. Outsiders tend to be acutely aware of their surroundings, as well as others' responses to their actions and words. And this makes them less able to unquestioningly engage: to take it in their stride. Such feelings start very young. Around 20 percent of toddlers experience early-life social sensitivity, which means – according to psychologist Daniel Goleman in his groundbreaking book *Emotional Intelligence* (1996) – they interact less, cry more, perceive threats more readily and are acutely shy with strangers.

And while half this group develop social competence by childhood, half remain 'behaviourally inhibited'. They may talk less, dislike domestic animals, refuse to eat new foods, and exhibit extreme reticence and withdrawal when meeting new people or even irregular contacts such as aunts and uncles. Even in adulthood, sensitive people become the wallflowers. They detest social situations while becoming 'morbidly afraid of having to give a speech or perform in public', says Goleman. So focused are they on their own sensitivity, they can also become insensitive to others' feelings.

And while some learn to overcome their timidity, others develop social anxiety that lasts a lifetime: always feeling on the edge of the group, socially anxious and alone in a crowd.

Cynicism. A chicken-and-egg propensity perhaps, but outsiders – by definition – observe things differently. We notice alternative aspects of a situation, usually more negative or troubling elements that others ignore (perhaps deliberately). This can work in our favour – as we'll explore later. But clan life likes conformity. So anyone spotting what shouldn't be spotted (perhaps what others are trying to hide), and vocalizing it, is likely to find themselves censured and potentially ostracized.

Of course, cynics may perceive and potentially exaggerate negativity. And that reinforces any nascent sense of distrust we feel towards others. Yet there's a wider concern with respect to distrust: that we're inwardly reacting to a sense of powerlessness. We look at societal structures and hate them simply because they feel like foreign impositions locking us out. And that makes us susceptible to conspiracy theories: to convictions that dark forces control our lives, which is a viewpoint unlikely to encourage integration.

Such an alternative view – seeing what others can't/won't – can (if removed of its extremism) be recognized for its entrepreneurial or creative potential (see Parts Two and Three). Yet that's no given. Usually, it's more darkness than daylight: meaning we drift further into the shadows until our negativity becomes a highly-disabling personality trait (more on negativity in Part Four).

Distorted empathy. Even trickier to confess is the fact such a distorted worldview can include empathizing with some of society's most unsavoury elements. Criminals, terrorists, even lone crazies shooting-up schools or shopping malls: outsiders can understand the mix of isolation, frustration and anger that can lead to such extreme acts, even if they're unlikely to execute the deed themselves.

For instance, I was living in America at the time of the 1999 Columbine High School massacre. Like everyone, I was shocked by the bloody scenes unfolding live on our office TV. Yet on hearing about Eric Harris's and Dylan Klebold's rage against 'the jocks' that dominated the school I understood their anger. Sure, the crime itself horrified me. But I 'got it' nonetheless.

Imposter syndrome. This may seem strange, given the above, but many outsiders are eager to be insiders. We bang on doors desperate to gain access to a group or club, membership of which – we assume – will positively change our outlook. Once beyond the threshold, however, we become quickly discomforted: a condition sometimes known as 'imposter syndrome'.

Psychologists Pauline Clance and Suzanne Imes discovered *imposter phenomenon* (as they label it) after interviewing highly-qualified women who complained, nonetheless, of feeling both out of their depth and not welcome as members of a (usually professional) grouping. The definition has since been expanded to embrace anyone who, having gained entrance on merit – no matter what the association – feels that they don't belong, perhaps due to unconscious convictions of unworthiness.

Interestingly, while the root cause may be due to feelings of unworthiness, we can mask our fears by expressing contempt or by emphasizing our lack of commonality with others in the group.

Certainly, boycotting the club – before it can reject us – is a classic ✓ outsider disposition, and certainly reflects my attitude to all those trendy London membership clubs.

Anger. Outsiders are often angry. Frustrated, an embittering sense of injustice can boil away inside us: meaning we rail against enemies seen and unseen, real or imagined. And the fact outsiders can go to the other extreme – being the detached, silent guy at the back of the room, saying nothing – doesn't disprove the point. It simply suggests some can suppress their inner turmoil while others openly rage against the machine.

Misunderstanding/feeling misunderstood. As we'll see, family pain is a major factor for outsiders. And family angst can come down to feeling misunderstood, which is often – though not always – the role of younger siblings. Most likely, outsiders are the younger 'laterborns' (see Chapter 3). Many grow up in an atmosphere of confusion – with conversations going on around them they only vaguely understand. Games are played and activities undertaken at the level of the older siblings, leaving the youngest confused and isolated.

In the maelstrom of family life, this can go unnoticed, meaning that our misunderstanding can result in feelings of being misunderstood. Such feelings can become ingrained, especially if younger siblings (as I was) are those born late in the academic year (yes, me again) and attend schools where class sizes result in scant individual attention (yessiree). Certainly, our family angst can be exacerbated, rather than alleviated, by what happens once within the school gates.

Of course, falling behind educationally is a quick way to develop an alternative perspective, which can also lead to behavioural issues that, ultimately, further separate us from the pack. Mind you, the same can be said for those too far ahead of their peers.

Dislike of authority. Outsiders are 'rebels without a cause'. We rail against any imposition of authority almost instinctively. Indeed, while outsiders can reveal inconsistent traits – we're true individuals after all – this one is something of a must. Authority gets up our nose.

As stated, I used to cheek the adults in the village, simply because they were adults. I disliked the teachers for the same reason, though this was mixed with convictions of being misunderstood. And I was even rebuked by the local policeman for being 'snotty' towards him. My contemporaries would stand back amazed as I answered back anyone trying to establish authority over me simply because they were older, or wore a uniform, or happened to own the land we were traversing.

Belief inconsistencies. Outsiders are lost souls, with no firm religious beliefs or guiding ideology to stabilize us, despite periodically making such a mental investment. As a result, we can become social and political butterflies: unable to consistently adopt any firm set of values or ideals. The beliefs we do fleetingly adopt, however, can be strongly held – perhaps due to an inner relief at having found a philosophical refuge from our mental chaos. Of course, cynicism soon sets in . . .

Yet this doesn't render us unprincipled. Outsiders can be highly moral people, despite – at times – indulging in immoral acts. Certainly, we have a moral compass that is well set and consistently pursued. That said, it has individualistic qualities that excuse personally-immoral behaviour such as drug-taking, sexual deviancy and even theft (especially when young).

Romanticism. As Holden Caulfield demonstrates, far from being contradictory, romanticism and cynicism can be a toxic mix for outsiders. It's almost indulgent – a hormonal wallowing in existential angst expressed through song or poetry, art or literature. Poetry suited best my tragic disposition, as well as my limited musical or artistic education. The same countenance that had me dolefully searching East End streets for sorrow had me drifting between 'greasy spoon' cafés: spending hours trying to note down meaningful rhyming couplets, though mostly just staring out the window pondering the sheer misery of it all.

Of course, such romanticism has a strong upside. We're both more creative and more adventurous (traits we'll explore in the pages ahead). The more remote something seems from the forces 'controlling' our lives, the more glamorous and alluring it appears, especially if there's an element of danger involved or an implicit rejection of 'normal' values. After all, both Hemingway and Orwell became embroiled in the Spanish Civil War – attracted, I suspect, as much by the war's romantic excitement as by the laudable fight against fascism.

Voyeurism and fantasy. Unfortunately, this feeling of being there but not being present – of watching rather than participating – can damage our sense of intimacy. For whatever reason, our ability to form mutual loving relationships can be impaired, which – in the digital age – can lead male outsiders (in particular) towards porn or gaming addiction, and both men and women towards fantasizing.

Porn suits the outsider's sense of voyeuristic 'otherness'. We're 'rubber neckers', fascinated by visually-shocking scenes such as accidents, crime and violence. But our voyeurism also taps into an ability to fantasize that's often misunderstood. Far from day-dreaming, outsiders are capable of mentally-occupying a parallel universe.

The 1963 film *Billy Liar* (based on a novel by Keith Waterhouse) reveals the inventive intensity of the fantasizing outsider. Billy Fisher (Tom Courtenay) lives his life within his own mental adventures, to the point that – challenged by one of his girlfriends Liz (Julie Christie) to run away to London – he claims to have escaped small-town Yorkshire long ago, for a world of his own making.

Could it be that the very 'otherness' that makes us outsiders also equips us with the creativity to, at least inwardly, escape (more on creativity in Part Three)?

Neurosis. There's no getting away from it, many outsiders are likely to be at least mildly neurotic. While able to function normally and appear well-adjusted enough for everyday life, we can exhibit a series of neurotic disorders including anxiety, sadness, depression, irritability and mental confusion.

According to American psychologist and leading personality-theorist C. George Boeree, the behavioural symptoms of the neurotic include 'phobic avoidance, vigilance, impulsive and compulsive acts, lethargy. . . . cognitive problems such as unpleasant or disturbing thoughts, repetition of thoughts and obsession, habitual fantasizing, negativity and cynicism'.

Many outsiders can tick off that list, for sure, though we must remember we're likely to occupy the less extreme ends of any neurosis spectrum.

Intolerance. And all the above can make the outsider someone intolerant of others' shortcomings, a list that can even include their seeming perfection. Our sensitivity can result in irritation and impatience – with noise, smells and visual distractions all capable of bothering us to an extent that amazes 'normal' people. Meanwhile, our distorted empathy makes others' successes hard to bear.

Perfectionism can follow: an intolerance of ourselves after setting perhaps unrealistic goals. And that can result in procrastination. Fearing the consequences of failure, we find excuses to delay execution, or make tiny amendments to a design or draft that prevents bold leaps forward. That said, procrastination can be equally the result of disliking outside pressure – with us digging in our heels against any imposition. As partners (in both love and work) we're impossible – difficult to manage and quick to criticize but also prone to taking offence at others' (perhaps perceived) criticisms of us.

Are we more intelligent, or less?

As stated, there's no *edge* offered in any of the above. Yet perfectionism and intolerance throw up an important question for outsiders: are we more intelligent than our peers, or less? Of course, it can be both. Certainly, we can perceive the world differently – maybe with a deeper level of insight. And we can excel in certain subjects, although this is usually more the result of nurturing than born 'genius'. Yet, equally, our feelings of 'otherness' can be due to falling behind. Formal education can be a struggle – for whatever reason – meaning we develop alternative routes for winning attention, or maybe seek our own stimulation well away from any formalized setting.

Either way, estrangement from our peers becomes ingrained – reinforced by both our reactions and their reactions to our actions. At some point in this self-confirming cycle our distance from the group becomes apparent. And it's then just a question of learning to accept our identity as an outsider.

The Outsiders' Checklist: *Are you an outsider? Well here's a (by no means comprehensive) checklist, though remember that outsiders are true individuals:*

- *Sensitivity*
- *Poor social competence*
- *Cynicism and negativity*
- *Distorted empathy (rooting for the bad guy)*
- *Imposter beliefs*
- *Anger and reactivity*
- *Detachment (sometimes masked by acting 'cool')*
- *Feeling misunderstood*
- *Misunderstanding (especially social) situations*
- *Dislike of authority*
- *Belief inconsistencies*
- *Romanticism*
- *Voyeurism*
- *Impaired intimacy*
- *Fantasy and other-worldliness*
- *Neurosis (including anxiety and depression)*
- *Intolerance and irritability*
- *Perfectionism*
- *Procrastination.*

The Outside *Edge*

obliged to take the feeli
hairy, forest-dwellin
Hunting there
ing decision-
cooperatio
Leade
hu

The trouble with reading I
Naked Ape (1967) is that, once read, it's difficult to view people as anything other than sophisticated monkeys. Yet – at least according to Morris and other sociobiologists – that's exactly what we are: monkeys, with outsidership no more than a facet of our evolutionary roots.

Nearly all primates are hierarchical, observes Morris – even tyrannical. Usually, the dominant males fight for singular control of the troop, with periodic changes of regime caused by the slowing of age, which opens up opportunities for the ambitious. As humans evolved, so autarchy developed to enforce hierarchy over greater numbers. And this led to the development of tribes, run by a monarch, which – in turn, and over millennia – led to the nation state: a societal structure requiring the collective buy-in of the entire colony.

The Paleolithic Age – a broad era lasting until as recently as 10,000 years ago – is the key period. It's here where collaborative, rather than tyrannical, hierarchical structures emerged, say the sociobiologists. The reason: the adoption of hunting (rather than simply foraging) as a means for feeding the group.

'Within the group the tyrannical hierarchy system of the usual primate colony had to be modified considerably to ensure full cooperation from the weaker members when out hunting,' writes Morris in *The Naked Ape*. 'There had to be a mild hierarchy, with stronger members and a top leader . . . even if this leader was

...gs of his inferiors more into account than his
... equivalent would have to do.'
...ore provides the basis for group endeavours requir-
...aking that relies upon mutually-agreed leadership and
... rather than just the despotism of the dominant male.
... would, as before, fight their way to the top. Yet, once there,
...ing required them to consolidate their power through alliance-
...uilding, patronage and generosity. Others in the group could either
accept this – perhaps angling for favour – plot rival alliances, or
leave.

This need for cooperation is the glue of tribalism, opines Morris, who also considers the growth of sophisticated hunting the root of religion and ceremony – acting, as it does, as a unifying force generating the required level of conformity across the clan and legitimacy in the clan's hierarchy. And from here a group's identity emerges. An identity, what's more, that brooks no questioning or individualism, simply because hunter-gatherer societies cannot afford to support individuals refusing to fall in with the accepted leader's plans for feeding and/or protecting the group. If that requires strict group behaviours and reverential adherence to fantastical rituals, so be it.

Yet, as societies prosper – generating a surplus – some individuals are likely to develop a wider outlook. They'll fail to integrate. The leadership of others may bother them – not always due to their own ambitions. Or they may question the legitimacy of those rituals. Cynicism follows, as does distorted empathy, frustration and, eventually, passive-aggressive or even outright rebellion: all the hallmarks of the classic outsider.

The rejected changeling

Yet rejection of the clan's hierarchy or tribal ritualism is not the whole story. Not by a long way. Outsiders are also society's rejects: perhaps those unable to meet the clan's standards in terms of genetic purity – a natural requisite in any biological grouping, although one that can be as much mental as physical.

For instance, throughout recorded history – and in nearly all societies – there's been the folklore legend of the changeling: of the child, swapped (usually at birth) by some mystical presence. These are often fairies or trolls or even the Devil. And they exchange the baby for one of their own, although disguise the swap by giving the interloper the same human form as the taken child.

A variety of motives have been attached to these spiritual trades – including old fairies needing a new body, baby fairies needing human milk or as part of a 'tithe to Hell'. And many attributes help identify them: often a small physical deformity or a mental impairment, with modern popular culture adding a few more (such as the 'number of the beast' in the 1976 suspense horror movie *The Omen*).

Of course, it's superstitious nonsense. Many 'changeling' children had little more than a minor facial blemish, although many more were simply slow developers, perhaps even autistic or with coordination issues such as dyspraxia. Some were no more than sensitive children unable to integrate into boisterous communal life.

Whatever the differentiation, it was enough to arouse suspicion, which led to them being treated differently – generating self-fulfilling behaviours that further alienated them from the group. The result: ostracism, shame, abuse and even murder. Indeed, believing some-one a changeling was cited as a defence for murder right into the nineteenth century.

The changeling myth is, of course, how medieval societies dealt with those that didn't integrate (for whatever reason) – by assuming they'd been possessed or even exchanged for another. Unfortunately, we see the echoes of these superstitions today – for instance, in the witchcraft accusations against African children. Heartbreakingly, in the Democratic Republic of Congo alone as many as 25,000 children scavenge an existence on the streets of the capital Kinshasa (according to a 2006 report in *The Observer*): all due to family rejection caused by witch accusations.

The battles of identity

Again, identity is the key. If you're not part of the group's identity, you're pushed to the edge: a phenomenon just as prevalent in developed countries today, without a witch, fairy or dominant male in sight. Yet identity is also a personal concern. It's how we're perceived and perceive ourselves in relation to the tribe (these days usually labelled 'society'): something that can drive a mental and even physical wedge between us and the wider world.

The German/American psychologist Erik Erikson (1902–94) became the world's greatest authority on identity – even coining the term 'identity crisis' when chronicling the mental battles of childhood development and their impact. In his 1968 work *Identity: Youth and Crisis*, Erikson described the cumulative effect of our developmental struggles by the time we reach adolescence: how, like a ship setting an incorrect course from the outset, we can find ourselves adrift from our fellow clansmen through a series of developmental either/or battles. Battles, what's more, that start the moment we're born and last right into adulthood (in fact, our entire life):

* From birth, Erikson describes our primary battle as one of *trust versus mistrust*. If nurtured in a safe, loving and predictable environment, we develop a sense of belonging. Meanwhile, inconsistent care – as any suspected changeling would certainly receive – results in a sense of abandonment, generating fear, suspicion and mistrust.
* Years one-to-three herald the next of Erikson's battles: *autonomy versus shame and doubt*. We become mobile, which fosters a sense of self and a need to explore. Yet repeated failures or ridicule – perhaps from older siblings or impatient parents – can generate shame and harm nascent confidence. Indeed, it's here where self-esteem issues first arise, although – again – the behavioural consequences of any self-esteem issues can separate us from the group.

- Years three-to-six, and we're developing physically, intellectually and socially, which brings about the clash of *initiative versus guilt*, says Erikson. We become curious and, if encouraged, learn to express ourselves. And that reinforces our sense of initiative. Irritated parents or teachers, meanwhile – perhaps telling us to 'stop showing off' – or maybe those overly-concerned by a child's safety, can kill initiative and suppress our sense of curiosity, which can result in a retreat into a private world.
- Moving on, years six-to-11 bring about the battle of *industry versus inferiority*. Peer approval now matters, and teachers or mentors assume significance – all reinforcing our feelings of acceptance or otherwise. Meanwhile, skill acquisition becomes a key concern, which can both support or challenge our self-esteem as well as our identity within the group.
- Which brings us to *identity versus role confusion,* the conflict emerging between the ages of 12 and 18. Adolescence – the transition from childhood to adulthood – is a period of profound change, making us ponder both who we are and what our potential future looks like. And this can generate what Erikson calls 'role confusion'. Ideas ferment and emotions explode – often in unpredictable ways. Who am I? Where do I belong? What's my role? – all questions bubbling away in an excited cauldron of potential and frustration.

Role confusion

Many – in fact most – youngsters slip into adult life without a murmur of complaint, even enthusiastically. They see a range of possibilities within established society, all of which are capable of accommodating their ambitions. Others don't: often those consistently on the more conflictual side of Erikson's dichotomies, as well as those previously ostracized for whatever reason. And this opens the door to further struggles with group integration – generating a sense of always seeking, but never finding, our true identity.

Role confusion follows, says Erikson. This is an inner struggle for understanding that has a profound impact in areas such as intimacy (where we struggle to sustain any form of mutual human bonding); time management (which prevents future planning); and industry (instead, focusing on irrelevant activities). To others we can look and sound like wastrels. Yet, within, we're battling anguish, fear and alienation.

Such maladjustment is the curse of adolescence, bringing with it what psychologists call 'non-normative' risks. These come thick and fast: dropping out of school, unemployment, sexually-transmitted diseases, teenage pregnancy, antisocial behaviour (including criminality), drug addiction, homelessness and even suicide. All spike between the ages of 15 and 20. Of course, the authorities know this and pay particular attention to this group, not always sympathetically – adding to our sense of alienation.

The identity journey

Certainly, many outsiders will have nodded along to Erikson's identity concerns. And other psychologists, such as Canada-based adolescence specialist James Marcia, may generate a similar response. Marcia built upon Erikson's work – stating that adult identity develops and settles only once we've journeyed through four distinct 'statuses'. Each involves various levels of 'exploration', 'crisis', or 'commitment', he states, and are:

* *Diffusion/confusion* – the least mature status in which we've barely started thinking about identity issues.
* *Foreclosure* – where we, usually prematurely, commit to an identity. This can be the result of peer group or parental pressure, or due to the lack of realistic or known alternatives.
* *Moratorium* – in which Erikson's identity crisis emerges, with us exploring alternative identities, often without success or with disillusionment quickly setting in.

- And *identity achievement* – where, having experienced crisis, we manage to successfully adopt a particular identity with its own customs, rules and values.

These are not necessarily developmental stages, says Marcia, meaning we can remain stuck in any particular 'status'. Yet most psychologists agree that – especially among young men – they're broadly age related. That said, it's the moratorium status of identity-experimentation that those battling with feelings of alienation can struggle to leave. As a result, many young outsiders indulge in 'identity hopping' – i.e. exploring a range of sometimes radical identities that are adopted and dropped in rapid succession.

The one in the ABC1 demographic

I certainly struggled with identity-hopping. It took marriage and a degree of economic security for me to settle on any form of identifiable identity, although – even then – it was more a negative acceptance of my non-identity than any wholesale adoption of something positive. In fact – and with apologies for the indulgence – my own battles with identity are worth outlining in order to reveal the sense of contradiction 'role confusion' can generate.

- My first identifiable identity was, as documented, *the bad boy*. This lasted right through junior school as I tried to ingratiate myself with other boys in the village by pushing the boundaries of acceptable behaviour – earning me the disapproval of the adults and teachers.
- Next came *the Cockney*. Now in senior school, I'd discovered and assumed my parents' (somewhat denied) East London heritage. I'd practice my rasping accent and wide-boy gait while learning rhyming slang with far greater gusto than I'd ever revised French verbs. I wholeheartedly adopted my father's rather weak football allegiances – even aligning (if not participating) with the team's renowned hooligan element.

- Extraordinarily, this was followed by *the intellectual*. Having left school at 16 (with one O-level) I opted for evening A-level classes, which – at last – opened my eyes to the power of education. Of course, I jumped right in: developing a 'gobshite' pseudo-intellectual persona, especially after I made it to university and integrated with the better-educated bohemians around me.
- Then there was *the eastern mystic*. A brief one, this – baggy clothes and long hair didn't suit me, although I enjoyed talking in that slow, nodding, 'yeah man' way and I became a dab hand at rolling my own cigarettes. But it felt so obviously like someone else's identity – making me a fake adopter of a fake identity – that it soon lost its appeal.
- And more career-minded identities were pressing upon me. After landing a role as a financial reporter I quickly became *the hard-boiled journo*. This involved being deeply cynical about everything (which I loved), a degree of misanthropy (ditto) and lots and lots of alcohol (yes, that too). For a period, I thought I'd found the vocation that suited my mental exile – an officially-sanctioned version of cheeking the grown-ups.
- But then something strange happened. I started enjoying hanging out with the bankers I was writing about. They had a strong insider-handle on the way the world worked and seemed cooler, more confident, and better dressed than us chippy-outsider journos. I wanted in, and grabbed an opening at one of the UK's leading investment banks. In fact, I became the *City Slicker* from central casting: red braces, brogues, pin-striped suit – striding down Bishopsgate bellowing into a mobile phone with all the 'master of the universe' brashness I could muster.
- Yet it just wasn't me – not least because I didn't have the maths skills required to hold my own in those ultra-competitive deal meetings. By this time, however, I was living in New York. I'd also filled out physically and my confidence with the opposite sex had grown (from an admittedly low base). So here came identity number seven: *the cheeky English rogue* in New York – out on the town pursuing sexual conquests like a rampant tomcat.

- This lasted two years, including a return to London and the publication of a 'lad lit' book on my exploits. Of course, the book did my banking career no favours, but I didn't care – not least because I'd discovered a new identity: *the posh boy*. Having met the woman that became my wife I was more than happy to adopt her identity. Yet my wife is quite posh. More North London/ *Guardian* posh than West London/Hampshire posh, admittedly – involving aesthetic rather than materialistic snobberies.
- As with banking, it was never me. So – approaching middle age – I finally take pride in being *the perennial outsider*: claiming I come from a social group of one (me!) and even joking that I'm the 'one' in those 'ABC1' demographic classifications. I live in one of only a handful of global cities that welcome identity-challenged misfits, and have used my innate entrepreneurialism (see Chapter 7) to establish my own public relations company – the industry most suited to those incapable of forging an identity of their own.

Highly-structured youth movements

Beyond revealing a classic inclination for introspection, what does listing my various identities reveal about outsiders? First, that our periodic attempts at identity adoption can involve full-on commitments. Each time, we mean it – thinking salvation awaits once within our new mental sanctuary. New values, new friends, a new look and wardrobe and even new living arrangements all form part of the mix, making role confusion and identity-hopping an expensive business.

And, second, that – apart from my brief brush with eastern mysticism – my identities all lacked the uniformity of a classic youth movement. This is especially intriguing given that the stereotypical image of an adolescent outsider is a black-wearing 'emo' (or its prior equivalents), while identity-hoppers surely flit between one standardized youth movement and another. It's also interesting because my extended youth – covering the late 1970s and 1980s

– offered probably the widest seam of alternative youth identities in history. Skinheads, rude boys, mods, headbangers, punks, goths, new romantics, soulboys/casuals, ravers and even crusties – all with their own distinct look, music and attitude.

Yet despite knowing people adopting each one of these identities, I steered clear for reasons obvious to genuine outsiders. As sub-cultures, they're all highly-structured groupings with their own hierarchies, rituals, values and iconography – all things likely to disturb the classic outsider grappling with Erikson's 'role confusion'.

Mistaken Identity

- *The development of hunting led to hierarchical structures built on more than mere tyranny – in fact, encouraging cooperation across the colony.*
- *This led to the development of group identities – a tribal glue that everyone was expected to adhere to.*
- *Inevitably, some rejected or were rejected by these identity-based cultural structures.*
- *But identity is also a personal battle – one generated in childhood and lasting into adulthood.*
- *Erikson's developmental battles culminate, in adolescence, with identity versus role confusion, which can lead to 'crisis'.*
- *'Identity-hopping' is a classic sign of crisis, in which we experiment with sometimes radically-different identities.*
- *Outsiders are rarely comfortable within standardized youth-tribe identities, again disliking the strict hierarchies and rituals.*
- *Ultimately, we have to accept that we're individuals, unable to adopt any group identity.*

3

ADOLESCENCE, FAMILY AND OPPORTUNITY

W e need to stay in adolescence for the moment because it's here where our outlook on life can become crystallized – the die seemingly cast as we move from childhood into adulthood. Reject or be rejected by the clan here, and a lifetime of alienation – of life on the edge – awaits.

Partly, and excruciatingly, this is due to the unmentionable but oh-so-important changes taking place to our body. Puberty – the physical and hormonal arrival of adulthood – generates much of the disorientation that young outsiders experience. And it's not just the onset of puberty that matters. Its timing also plays a pivotal role in determining feelings of maladjustment and alienation.

Psychologists talk about 'normative' and 'non-normative' elements to puberty. 'Normative maturational shifts' are both physical and obvious: including growth spurts, breast-development and menstruation for girls; and growth spurts, genital growth and sperm production for boys. Both develop pubic hair, while boys also develop facial hair.

'Non-normative maturational shifts', meanwhile, are brought about by the psychological disruption of adulthood's onset, as well as having to concurrently cope with external pressures such as heightened educational expectations and exacerbated family tension. Previously well-adjusted kids may clash with those around them – generating conflict and estrangement from their once close family and peers. Thrill-seeking behaviour, eating disorders, extreme feelings of disadvantage (even victimhood) can follow – rooted, say psychologists, in the mental chaos generated by the physical changes underway.

Certainly, puberty can foster a spectrum of intense psychological responses: low self-esteem and self-hatred at one end; over-confidence and even arrogance at the other – feelings that, over time, separate us from the clan. What's interesting for our purposes, however, is that among the factors generating this separation are the non-normative responses triggered by either the early, or late, onset of puberty. The comparative timing of puberty, it turns out, can be critical for the development of the outsider.

The timing of puberty

Puberty's timing is extraordinarily varied. For some it arrives as early as nine or 10 (particularly for girls). And, for others, it concludes as late as 17–18 (usually a male concern) – with either end of the scale generating a physical differentiation from our peers with deep psychological consequences. The sequence of events can also vary. For instance, menstruation for girls can be the first or last thing to happen, with both results leading to anxiety and, potentially, self-hatred. Likewise, with boys, growth spurts can come early or late and sperm production and ejaculation can be delayed – potentially until after becoming sexually active.

Yet growth spurts, genital development and pubic hair are all physical changes – making the differentiation visual (at least in the school changing rooms) and therefore highly comparative. For early-developing males in particular, this can be advantageous, which can – again – generate a sense of separation from contemporary peers. More normally, however – and especially for late developers – the response is to become self-critical of the changes underway (or not, as the case may be).

Studies by psychologists, including Anne C. Petersen and Lisa J. Crockett, back this up – concluding that the most marked psychological impacts of puberty on adolescents are seen on those deviating from their peers in terms of puberty's arrival. This is known as 'deviance hypothesis', with those who are off-time becoming more socially deviant than their peers. Early-maturing girls are the prime suspects in this respect – not least because girls can start puberty up to two years ahead of boys – followed by late-maturing boys.

Critically, the concept of deviance is entirely dependent on the peer-group circumstances. For instance, one study (by J. Brooks-Gunn and M.P. Warren in 1985) showed that girls maturing on time at a dance school became stressed and anxious – developing deviant behaviour such as personality and eating disorders. Meanwhile, those maturing late – and therefore retaining the 'perfect' low body weight for dancing – were less likely to exhibit deviant behaviour.

A supportive concept to 'deviance hypothesis' is what psychologists Roberta G. Simmons and Dale A. Blyth call 'cultural ideals' in which each culture – and even micro-culture (such as a dance school) – admires a perfect male and female physique. And while those able to meet this ideal have an *edge* over their peers – and are therefore more emotionally stable and confident – those falling short develop emotional problems and suffer from low confidence.

Late-maturing men that fail to develop the stature or build of the 'ideal' male – as well as early-maturing women that may become stressed due to weight gain – can therefore become depressed and socially detached from their peer group, which can lead to deviant behaviour. What's more, Simmons and Blyth state that the cultural, often glamorous, media stereotypes of the modern age tend to be internalized by youngsters and then used to provide a usually negative comparison.

Indeed, both those that match the ideal (taller boys, say) and those that don't (larger girls, perhaps) can develop a sense of being apart from their peers.

The disadvantaged outsider

One last point on maturation rates. While it's the outliers at both ends of the spectrum that develop a sense of distance from the group, the consequences vary greatly for those maturing early or late. As stated, males maturing early develop a considerable *edge* over their peers as they're able to socialize with older groups. They can, if desired, enter bars and clubs with over-18 restrictions and become sexually-active earlier – perhaps with older females – distancing themselves from their peers through their available choices.

And that brings up an interesting point about Holden Caulfield. From my adult reading of *The Catcher in the Rye*, there's little doubt Caulfield reached puberty early, which means his alienation is at least partly due to being physically out of kilter with his schoolboy status. He saw himself as too grown up to mix with his school contemporaries – hence trying to blag drinks in Midtown hotels.

Even more interesting – at least for my own outsider convictions – is the lie this gives my assumption that the differences between Caulfield and I were based on social status. His Midtown forays, compared to my East End skulks, could have had more to do with the physical, rather than social, gap between us. He reached maturation early while I was late – struggling to gain entrance to bars and nightclubs even at 18. And surely, this had a major impact on my confidence. Certainly, it affected my options when wandering the big city as an adolescent.

Of course, this potentially bursts my class bubble (at least in part). Yet it certainly confirms my earlier notion that there are two types of outsider: those distancing themselves from the group due to their advantages and choices – indeed, their *edge* – and those (I suspect more numerous) developing a sense of removal due to their disadvantages.

It's these two routes that – for me – explain the myth (peddled by Gladwell *et al.*) that the advantages of being an outsider outweigh the disadvantages. Just maybe those with an *edge* distance themselves from the clan due to their available choices, while the disadvantaged have outsidership thrust upon them.

The impact of self-esteem

Another element likely to come into play for the disadvantaged outsider is self-esteem, which – according to Melanie Fennell in her highly-regarded work *Overcoming Low Self-Esteem* (1999) – 'refers to the overall opinion we have of ourselves, how we judge or evaluate ourselves, and the value we attach to ourselves as people'.

If our self-view is that of a weak, inadequate or inferior person, writes Fennell, or if we're troubled by uncertainty and self-doubt, meaning we're unkind or critical about ourselves – perhaps feeling we lack true worth or any entitlement to the good things in life – then we suffer from low self-esteem.

As Erik Erikson explains in Chapter 2, feelings of inferiority or low self-esteem usually arise in infancy, perhaps due to parental or peer rejection. Yet there's another potential root: having too-elevated an 'ideal self'. Here, we've created an unbridgeable gap between our aspirations and our potential for attainment. And that undermines our self-worth.

This view comes from an equally renowned self-esteem specialist, Michael Argyle, writing in his 1967 tome *The Psychology of Interpersonal Behaviour*. And while this, again, brings in the disconcerting notion of 'cultural ideals', it also means that self-esteem issues can arise whenever comparisons become critical: when starting a new school for instance, but especially during the sexual awakening of puberty as well as the moment we first go out into the wider world as a fully-formed adult.

So, while early-life parental relationships are crucial for the development (or otherwise) of self-esteem, later concerns – such as peer group or cultural comparisons around puberty – can psychologically harm previously undamaged children. They can also generate a sense of alienation in those that once appeared well-adjusted to clan life.

Girls change friends, boys retreat

Gender's also relevant. Argyle points out that, while pubescent female agonies are acute, women appear better than men at sustaining their self-esteem through adolescence and young adulthood 'based mainly on harmonious relations with others'.

Given girls' famed social media feuds this may seem unlikely. Yet girls tend to remain collegiate – with groups forming and reforming constantly, although perhaps via disruptive fallouts and even via individual girls forming stronger bonds with boys (the 'tomboy' being a classic female outsider persona). Boys, meanwhile, can find themselves outcast and isolated – sometimes involuntarily, but often as a voluntary response to the challenges they face within peer groups.

Of course, Argyle was writing in the 1960s, meaning his view on gender differences may need updating. Yet there's certainly some truth in the notion that boys will more likely isolate themselves than girls. And with respect to other social divides – such as ethnicity – Argyle's on firmer ground.

'Self-esteem is *not* any lower among members of racial or other minority groups subjected to discrimination,' he writes, 'probably because it depends on the evaluation of, and comparisons with, individuals in the same group.'

That said, self-esteem issues can arise for ethnic minorities living within mixed communities because their ethnicity compared to their peers, makes them stand out as 'deviant' from the group norm. And – insists Argyle – self-esteem can be greatly affected by social class, reinforcing the notion that disadvantaged outsiders have an uphill struggle compared to their advantaged brethren.

Family scripts

And then there's our 'family script', which can have an impact on both our self-esteem and our propensity for developing an outsider mentality. My father spent my childhood openly favouring my older sister while denigrating my every utterance, which certainly impacted my self-esteem as a teen and young adult. In an effort to please him it also affected my early career choices, although this eventually resulted in me abandoning my family's values entirely – including pursuing my own goals in careers they barely understood.

Far from an abnormal result, psychologists such as Oliver James would call this the typical 'script' of the laterborn child. James, in his popular work on family survival *They F*** You Up* (2002), studied how the position of children within the family hierarchy had a significant impact on their outlook, as well as their feelings of commonality within the modern nuclear family.

Firstborn children, he noted, tend to express the core attitudes and convictions of the family, although have to deal with the 'shock' of lost attention when siblings arrive. That said, they're rewarded with greater responsibility early on, which can result in a cautious and conservative child that becomes well-integrated into family values.

Meanwhile, laterborns develop outsider attitudes such as risk-taking and a sense of adventure. They have to fight for attention from a disadvantaged position so become the rule-breakers – especially when there are lots of siblings, making the battle that much harder. Many go to great lengths to distinguish themselves. Many, also, develop more radical, even revolutionary, views. Leon Trotsky, Karl Marx and Fidel Castro – James notes – were all laterborn siblings, as was evolutionary (and revolutionary) scientist Charles Darwin.

Being laterborn is not the only family script that can lead to feelings of separation from the nuclear family unit, however. According to James, other influences include:

Beauty. While studies show that parents favour more beautiful children – doting on them at the expense of their less attractive siblings – good-looking children also develop a greater sense of independence. Both family and non-family adults take more interest in them, are kinder to them and forgive their misbehaviour more readily. As they develop, they tend to be more trusted and more listened to – with many good-looking adults becoming successful salespeople, as well as more likely fraudsters. Meanwhile, those

siblings having to witness such favouritism can develop a detachment from the family unit – again, showing the advantaged/
disadvantaged split in terms of routes to outsidership.

Grandparental indulgence. Immediate parents may work hard to
maintain a balance between siblings, which can be undermined by
extended family members such as grandparents or aunts. They may
openly favour particular offspring, again generating the advantaged/
disadvantaged divide: with the indulged kid potentially becoming
more independent or – perhaps more likely – the unfavoured sibling
feeling alienated due to the insensitivity of the grandparents.

Early loss. The childhood loss of one parent is a strong signifier
for early achievement, says James – with double the average of
both UK prime ministers and US presidents experiencing early
parental loss. The same statistic seems to work in business and
the arts, as well as philosophy and science – all areas requiring
unique thoughts and abilities for reaching the top. Initial reactions to
parental loss are problematic, however. Rage, distrust, alienation,
feelings of inadequacy and self-loathing: all generating an intense
battle for independent mastery that can lead to over-achievement,
antisocial behaviour and – again – radicalism. Indeed, revolution-
aries tend to have experienced early loss, which is combined with
extremism and distorted empathy to produce some of history's most
ruthless tyrants: Hitler, Stalin, Napoleon, Robespierre and Idi Amin
among them (more on extremism in Part Four).

The dilemma of choice

Yet hang on a minute! Sure, self-esteem is important when determining the poor outcomes of disadvantaged outsiders. And our family
scripts are relevant for formulating our general outlook. But it's
difficult to ignore the fact that the modern world presents choices
previous generations would have considered impossible. Surely,
feelings of alienation are just as much a consequence of the myriad
opportunities available within our wealthy, consumerist, society.

Quite possibly, it's not the lack of opportunity that's turning us into outsiders. It's the abundance.

Just as we dismissed Lou Reed's and Holden Caulfield's role confusion as the outcome of privileged choice, so we must accept that choice has become increasingly democratized. Yet these very choices exaggerate both the possible outcomes of rejectionist feelings of 'not belonging', and their likelihood. Indeed, this is even true of those blunted by the disablement of a second-rate education. As I proved through evening A-level classes, those lacking the advantages of educational privilege can still prosper – exploring openings and opportunities not open to earlier generations.

Subsistence societies – from hunter-gatherers right up to the bucolic and overly-romanticized farmers of pre-industrial societies – had no room for role confusion. Instead, the imperatives of life resulted in outsiders being quickly ostracized as troublemakers, with artistic eccentricity the near-exclusive preserve of those with the time and wealth for such indulgences. This was a tiny minority until the growth of the middle classes in the nineteenth century – hence the first rejectionist youth identity being the distinctly upper-crust *Romantic Movement* of the early 1800s. Now, however, the poetic discomforts of identity crisis and role confusion have become available to those either unable or unwilling to work.

The statistics prove it. As England's industrial age accelerated (say, around 1850), average life expectancy for men was 43 years (or 48 for those making it past their tenth birthday) compared to 78.4 years now – allowing for a considerably-extended adolescence. Meanwhile, the average worker toiled for well over 60 hours a week, compared to under 40 hours now – generating ever-lengthening leisure time (however wastefully consumed). Male farm labourers earned on average eight shillings a week (that's 40p) while a loaf of bread cost around a shilling, compared to a current weekly wage averaging £510 and supermarket bread costing as little as 50p.

Such affluence doesn't simply add choice, however. It adds pressure. If we're free to choose the skills and knowledge we acquire,

we're also free to determine our own paths towards personal fulfilment. Society places no limits on our potential in this respect,
although – for sure – some operate from more advantageous starting
points than others.

Yet this very abundance is a trap. Our freedom to succeed is also
our freedom to fail, which adds to the stress. Of course, we can reject
this – perhaps choosing to 'opt out' or pursue creative rather than
materialistic goals. But, even here, affluence has resulted in the
packaging of rebellion into a highly-developed route for success.
We're now so wealthy that rebellion has become rewarding – with
even recalcitrant graffiti artists such as Banksy producing highly-
valued work. As Andy Warhol, Johnny Rotten and Tracey Emin
have all demonstrated, rebellion's now a highly-packaged – and
profitable – rules-based form of self-expression with its own etiquette, hierarchies, snobberies and celebrities.

Rousseau's discourse of the vanities

Indeed, the very abundance of the modern world – all that freedom
and choice and life full of 'bucket lists' and sensual delights – can
generate an acute and highly-isolating fear of failure that can
exaggerate any nascent sense of alienation. Wealth – in all its forms
and however measured – can create profound unhappiness, something French philosopher Jean-Jacques Rousseau (1712–78) warned
against in the eighteenth century.

Sometimes described as the high-priest of Romanticism, Rousseau –
writing in his *Discourse on the Origin of Inequality* (1754) – states
that wealth (including spiritual wealth) is purely relative. It's a state
of having what we desire. If we want something we cannot afford,
we're poor, no matter what our resources for acquiring other goods.
On the other hand, when we're satisfied with what we have, we're rich.
This is certainly true with private wealth, although it's also true of
other human distinctions such as skill, creativity or, these days,
notoriety.

He describes it thus:

'It became customary to gather in front of the huts: song and dance . . . became the amusement. . . . Everyone began to look at everyone else and to wish to be looked at himself, and public esteem acquired a price. The one who sang or danced best; the handsomest, the strongest, the most skilful, or the most eloquent came to be the most highly regarded, and this was the first step towards inequality and vice: from these first preferences arose vanity and contempt on the one hand, shame and envy on the other . . . compounds fatal to happiness and innocence.'

For Rousseau, the best way to feel rich is not to gain more but to want less – perhaps by distancing one's self from anybody we consider 'rich'. Of course, such distancing can be mental as well as physical. It can be the adoption of values that openly reject the pressures of 'wealth creation', however we define wealth. Yet, as we've seen, that doesn't end the pressure. New pressures and vanities emerge that look remarkably like the old ones.

So while Rousseau foresaw both the inequalities and snobberies that industrial wealth would produce, he couldn't have foreseen that even his recommended way out – the adoption of rejectionist values and alternative lifestyles – would generate the same pressures (although it became quickly apparent within the *Romantic Movement*).

Little wonder so many people feel like outsiders.

Puberty Blues

- *Puberty is a key moment for crystallizing our integration – or otherwise – into society.*
- *The late or early onset of puberty is a critical factor for generating feelings of disadvantage or alienation.*
- *Early maturing girls and late maturing boys are the most vulnerable to 'non-normative' responses and detachment – not least because of their deviance from cultural ideals.*

- *Self-esteem issues are another factor. Our self-esteem can be harmed in adolescence if we fail to live up to an 'ideal self'.*
- *'Family scripts' are also important. For instance, laterborn children may develop greater risk-taking attitudes and are more likely to adopt radical views – partly to affirm their individuality.*
- *Beauty, family favouritism and the early loss of a parent can all generate feelings of being separate, as can witnessing favouritism in siblings.*

4

EXISTENTIALISM AND THE NEED FOR A PURPOSE

Start researching outsiders, and it's not long before the word 'existentialism' crops up. Indeed, it crops up so often it cannot be ignored. Nor should it be because, within this rather tricky-to-define philosophical movement, lies potential salvation for outsiders. Not as reformed insiders, I hasten to add, but as mental exiles on our own terms – developing an *edge* while pursue meaningful objectives.

In fact, existentialism is more an attitude than a philosophy – at least according to American academic Robert C. Solomon in his key work *Existentialism* (1974). An attitude, what's more, that emanates from the sense of disorientation we face on realizing life's apparent meaninglessness. Indeed, existentialism is a disposition nearly all outsiders can embrace. It's angst unravelled and examined; it's cynicism legitimized; and it's alienation put in its rightful place at the centre of our motivation.

Certainly, if you've ever wondered about the meaning of life or asked 'What's the point of it all?' – perhaps while mournfully staring out of a café window – you've been pondering existentialism. Existentialists attempt to make sense of the pain, confusion and even the absurdity of human life. Intensity rather than serenity is what matters to the existentialist: truth rather than happiness. They're also interested in the individual, rather than the group or 'mankind' in general – something that suits outsiders' inherently self-absorbed take on the world.

Yet, despite flirting with ideas such as suicide, it's far from nihilistic (the conviction that life has no value). This is good news for outsiders because – while existentialism was pitching itself against formalized religion in the nineteenth century – its more contemporary battle is with the 'just enjoy yourself' shallowness of modern hedonism. These days, existentialists are the intense-looking guys too often being told to 'chill out' or to 'stop taking life too seriously'.

Oh yes, existentialism's our kind of philosophy alright.

Hegel's contradictions

Danish philosopher Søren Kierkegaard (1813–55) is considered the godfather of the existentialists, although things really hot up for outsiders with the late nineteenth-century arrival of Friedrich Nietzsche (1844–1900) – the much misunderstood inventor of the 'superman' or 'übermensch'. And, of course, there's Jean-Paul Sartre – the movement's rock star.

But let's not jump the gun because Sartre and especially Nietzsche only make sense after Kierkegaard, who only makes sense after Georg Wilhelm Friedrich Hegel (1770–1831), who was criticizing enlightenment-philosopher Immanuel Kant (1724–1804). Such is the way with philosophers.

Stuttgart-born Hegel was a secret atheist or – at least – a cynic of the highly-religious German society of his time. His interest in God was in how spiritual concepts manipulated a human's view of the world, which he rationalized into a series of contradictions or opposites that we spend our lives battling. These include hypothetical conflicts between the *general* and the *specific* and the *finite* and the *infinite*. But they also include more 'existential' contradictions – such as those between *God* and *man*, *good* and *bad*, *bondage* and *freedom* – that are a strong fit for Erikson's identity battles discussed in Chapter 1.

According to Hegel, these antagonisms are always subject to change. It's what makes human consciousness an evolving process, based on 'dialectical' reasoning (philosopher-speak for rational debate). And it refutes Kant's belief in an unchanging framework of governing principles.

These antagonistic battles never end, says Hegel. Indeed, harmony's not the aim, which is for each conflict to seek resolution before moving on to the next battle. For instance, the notion (or 'thesis' in Hegelese) of *tyranny* brings with it the opposite idea (or 'antithesis') of *freedom*, which creates a middle way (or 'synthesis') of *law* (a framework for controlling *freedom* while preventing *tyranny*). Thus man evolves.

Yet each resolution or synthesis throws up a new thesis/antithesis conflict, requiring (after much debate) another middle-way synthesis. And while this looks like a continuous and exhausting round of aggravation, it generates progress. Of course, Hegel describes well the evolution of the species, and many see a close correlation between Hegel's contradictions and Charles Darwin's theory of evolution. Yet it also describes the centuries-old battle against injustice and inequality – as well as, and importantly for outsiders, our antagonisms as individuals. Our inner conflicts are both inevitable and necessary, considers Hegel, because they lead to resolution, though one full of new antagonisms.

Hegel thus explains our mental anguish. Outsiders are life's thinkers – aware of the contradictions and compromises and keen to explore and explain them rather than pretend 'everything's fine'. And we're prepared to pursue this quest no matter how miserable it makes us. *Good for us!*

Kierkegaard adds a moral dimension

For Hegel, these antagonisms lead to resolutions determined by the historical or environmental or even social conditions we face. They also follow a path of inevitability – a notion Søren Kierkegaard refutes. While happy to take up and run with Hegel's baton of earthly antagonistic choice, the poetic outsider Kierkegaard (best quote: 'People understand me so little that they do not even understand when I complain of being misunderstood') believes that our lives are determined by *our* actions. Actions, what's more, that are based on the moral choices we make and not on factors that are beyond our control.

Forget our childhood issues and poor conditioning, contends the great Dane. Our decisions are ours to make now, in real-time. Nothing is inevitable. We have free will. So we can either opt for the hedonistic self-gratifying choice – or, come to that, for the self-justification of being miserable – or we can opt for something more wholesome.

Interestingly, Kierkegaard assumes we innately understand our own free will, hence our anxiety – even dread – when faced with important decisions. For instance, in his book *The Concept of Anxiety* (1844) he observes that, if we stand at the cliff's edge, we experience two concerns: one is of falling, while the other is the impulse to jump. We can choose to plunge to our death – something Kierkegaard calls the 'dizziness of freedom'.

So the need to make terrifying decisions generates anxiety, which can induce despair, says Kierkegaard: feelings outsiders can certainly relate to. Yet it can also shake us from our unthinking responses by making us aware of the available choices. Balance is the key – a Hegelian synthesis between necessity and possibility. We can drown in life's necessities but we can also be driven mad by a surfeit of possibilities, considers Kierkegaard, an affliction he assumes is the curse of modern (i.e. mid-nineteenth century) man.

For Kierkegaard the answer's obvious: search for a life with meaning and purpose (a theme we'll return to again).

'We are all too human,' says Nietzsche

Laissez-faire live-and-let-live attitudes are, of course, anathema for outsiders, although the fight for nineteenth century existentialists wasn't against the 'why worry?' agnosticism of twenty-first century hedonism. It was against the prevalent religious doctrine that what happens in this life is less important than the next.

This, for existentialists such as Friedrich Nietzsche, is abandoning life itself.

'God is dead,' declared Nietzsche, by which he meant that life isn't a forerunner to a more important existence after death. Our higher values – even our morality – shouldn't come from some external power but from within. He thought that man's reliance on religion and even on the spiritual was our 'longest philosophical error' – a revolutionary attitude in the nineteenth century.

'Where you see ideal things, I see things which are only human, alas all-too-human,' writes Nietzsche in *Human, All Too Human* (1878). 'I know man *better* – the term "free spirit" must here be understood in no other sense than this: a freed man, who has once more taken possession of himself.'

Born near Leipzig in 1844, and raised the son of a country parson, Nietzsche predicted the philosophical crisis to befall mankind due to the loss of religious 'truth'. Instead, he saw the individual human as the sole measure of his or her freedom and worth – making Nietzsche, by his own reckoning, the first 'modern man'.

Without God, he pondered, we must take charge of our own moral destinies – discovering the difference between good and evil, right and wrong. For Nietzsche, this was a bitter-sweet disposition. Human suffering makes no sense without religion, he reasoned. Yet religion prevents us from discovering the real, objective, truth.

Rise of the superman

Yet Nietzsche was always willing to question his own assumptions. To take a fresh look. He saw himself as the lonely wanderer tackling the big questions – eventually even adopting the life of a hermit in the Swiss Alps.

Ultimately, mental and physical illness – then attributed to the burden of his philosophical enquiries, although more likely to have been syphilis – took its toll on Nietzsche and his writings became somewhat manic. He stated that 'man is something that shall be overcome' – meaning that we must transcend our own moral frailties: developing, in time, into a 'superman' or '*übermensch*'.

'What is the ape to man?' he asked in *Thus Spoke Zarathustra* (1885) a philosophical novel and parable to explain the death of God. 'A laughing stock or a painful embarrassment. And man shall be just that for the *übermenschen*: a laughing stock or a painful embarrassment.'

At heart, the *übermensch* proposes the ideal individual: over-coming emotional and physical barriers while guided by their own principles into achieving their greatest possible self. It's a battle of self-mastery in which we – as part of our human duty – rise above our humdrum limitations: forging our *edge* in the process.

Of course, the *übermensch* can be misinterpreted, and was twisted by the Nazis to support their Aryan-supremacy ideology, not helped by Nietzsche's sister posthumously reinterpreting his writing to suit her political sympathies. Yet this is to miss a vital message for outsiders. Nietzsche's plea is to develop and pursue our own moral quest: a personal, individual, mission – devoid of God – and nothing to do with race or class or gender.

'Throw off your discontent about your nature,' he wrote in *Human, All Too Human*. 'Forgive yourself your own self. You have it in your power to merge everything you have lived through – false starts, errors, delusions, passions, your loves and your hopes – into your goal, with nothing left over.'

Just as Nietzsche's own 'muck' (his description for his rambling thoughts and experiences) had to be turned into the philosophical gold of his writings, so we have to transcend our own ordinary, painful, experiences and past mistakes to find our personal 'truth'.

In this respect, Nietzsche's underlying message becomes totemic for the outsider. Simply put, we must seek our own 'truth': one giving us our unique *edge*.

We must define ourselves

So where does the thinker most closely associated with existentialism come in? In fact, Jean-Paul Sartre (1905–80) – the movement's poster-boy – has outsider written all over him. This small (5'2"), half-blind Protestant (in a Catholic country) lost his father aged two, detested his step-father and failed to bond with his school contemporaries. He felt like a fish out of water at university – the prestigious *École Normale Supérieure* – and was laughed at for his poor physicality on joining the French army at the start of World War Two.

Even his German captors released him as 'unfit for active service' – resulting in him spending the war years writing and staging surreptitiously insubordinate plays in occupied Paris. Hating 'bourgeois' conformity and any form of collective morality, he refused to join either of France's post-war leftwing political parties, membership of which was considered *de rigueur* for French intellectuals at the time. He also condemned both church and state for their assumed right to judge others, hated the French middle-classes for their absurd snobberies and was disgusted by the righteous convictions of the elite.

Sartre offered an alternative view to the collective assemblies of church, state or party: the individual. For him, each person was the absolute master of his or her conscience – hence Sartre's redemptive qualities for the outsider. Yet his qualities go far beyond redemption. How's this for a quote to contemplate while staring out of the café window:

'Everything that exists is born for no reason, carries on living through weakness and dies by accident,' he wrote in the novel *Nausea* (1938).

Sartre's our man, alright – not least because he also offers us a way out.

'Man is fully responsible for his nature and his choices,' wrote Sartre, adding: 'As far as men go, it is not what they are that interests me, but what they can become.'

Existentialist angst is no excuse for isolation. It's a call for engagement: for developing into our greatest potential expression.

Sartre's key point is that, with respect to humans, 'existence precedes essence'. While tools such as scissors or a spade have their form dictated by their function, humans have no specific function other than to exist. So we're free to shape ourselves – to develop our unique form: our *edge*.

'First of all man exists,' he writes in *Existentialism is a Humanism* (1946), 'turns up, appears on the scene, and only afterwards defines himself.'

Condemned to be free

So while we must pursue our own goals – shaping our own lives – there's nothing within us forcing us to do this. Being a couch potato is no less human than striving for moral or physical perfection, considers Sartre. Yet Sartre doesn't release us from the need to pursue meaningful lives. His treatise is not nihilistic – a 'what's the point?' philosophy that allows us to spend our lives pursuing a hedonistic release that blunts our potential. We're 'condemned to be free,' he says.

And that freedom brings with it moral obligations. We must make it happen – for instance, engaging politically to question or even remove authoritarian structures, in whatever form.

'With freedom comes responsibility,' is not Sartre's quote (it's Eleanor Roosevelt's). But it's Sartre's sentiment. We're responsible for our own outcomes. No higher power will save us. Nothing is preordained. Yet from this chaos we can choose our own path, which – while selfish – is far from meaningless: we owe it to ourselves to both ask the questions and pursue the answers, no matter how miserable this makes us.

After the totalitarian nightmares of the 1930s and 1940s, this was a powerful message – and one that inspired the Paris student revolt of May 1968. Sartre – a revolutionary and hero of the left – attacked the role of the Communists in the revolt as essentially authoritarian and conservative. The Communists feared change, he said, while Sartre embraced revolution – a permanent revolution in which every successful change opens up new battles (echoing Hegel).

Sartre wanted a revolution based on individual freedom and expression, which contradicted his declared Marxism – something he admitted in later years. Yet his answer was to become more extreme, even espousing terrorism as the 'atomic bomb of the poor'. He became 'a rebel with a thousand causes,' to quote the *New York Times* obituary, 'a modern Don Quixote'.

An outsider to the last.

Indifference and meaninglessness

A final existentialist worth mentioning is Albert Camus (1913–60) – a French-Algerian brought up in poverty, and author of a novel actually called *The Outsider* (at least in English: *L'Etranger* in French). It's a miserable narrative that opens with the line: 'Mother died today. Or maybe yesterday; I can't be sure.'

The protagonist, Meursault, sums up Camus's outlook by expressing no grief or regrets – just detached indifference – through death, infidelity, murder and his own impending execution.

'There is only one really serious philosophical problem, and that is suicide,' declares Camus. 'Deciding whether or not life is worth living is to answer the fundamental question in philosophy.'

Life is banal and pointless, says Camus. And our search for meaning absurd – contesting Nietzsche's and Sartre's certainty that we can find life's substance.

'We are all condemned to death,' concludes the fictional Meursault as he awaits execution – Camus's position encapsulated in a sentence, and confirmed by his own absurd and senseless death aged 46 as a passenger is a car smash (despite possessing a train ticket for the journey).

In *The Myth of Sisyphus* (1942) Camus portrays life as a man permanently condemned to the futile task of pushing a rock uphill, although he also concludes that such a struggle can lead to fulfilment and even happiness. Indeed, Camus's view is that happiness is only possible once we accept life's meaninglessness, making Camus perhaps the purist existentialist of all, although also the thinker we must refute.

By taking existentialism to its logical conclusion – that life's absurd – Camus offers no salvation for the outsider. Sure, he assumes happiness can be found through mental surrender: perhaps leading to hedonistic wastefulness, even if disguised by the delusionary pursuit of seemingly-worthy goals such as 'travel' and 'experiences'. Yet such options are unavailable to cynical outsiders. We'd spot the touristic conveyor-belt of 'discovery' and extract little comfort from the experience, other than an insight into our own insignificance.

Yet Camus is spectacularly countered by one of my philosophical heroes: Viktor Frankl (1905–97). While sometimes branded an existentialist thinker, Frankl was actually an Austrian psychiatrist, as well as an expert on suicide: skills that came in handy after 1942 when Frankl and his entire family were deported (via a Czech ghetto) to the Nazi concentration camps. Only Frankl lived to tell the tale, which he did by writing one of the most powerful books of the twentieth century – at least from an angst-ridden outsider's point of view.

Man's Search for Meaning (1946) offers the most extraordinary insight: that our suffering – no matter how deep – ceases once it's given meaning. From watching fellow inmates succumb and die – many through suicide, despite Frankl's best attempts to prevent it – rather than endure the hopelessness of camp life, Frankl became determined to report his observations on the human condition under extreme stress. His wretched life now had meaning, he realized. And this made him determined to survive. It also gave him a perspective on his experiences that offered him far greater freedom than that of his captors.

While enduring camp hardships, Frankl imagined himself giving lectures on his experiences, allowing him to objectify himself and see his suffering from a distance. And it's this same objectivity that Frankl implores us to find. One that allows us to give our suffering (however expressed) meaning – probably the most powerful message outsiders can possibly hear.

Forget pondering life's meaning while staring out of the café window, *get out there and find it*: Kierkegaard, Nietzsche, Sartre and Frankl all insist that we do.

It's also the perfect riposte to Camus's view of the absurdity of life. Nothing's less absurd than a life with meaning. Indeed, the search for meaning is what will give the disadvantaged outsider their *edge*, although – as Frankl states – this isn't something you can invent. It's something you must discover, which is our task for Part Two.

10 Things Existentialists Teach Outsiders

Yet, as outsiders, we may already be distancing ourselves from existentialism – perhaps thinking it too abstract or that the declaration 'God is dead' too dogmatic. So below is existentialism's key lessons for the outsider.

1. Life can indeed seem pointless, even absurd. So our central need is to discover whether life's worth living.
2. For Hegel, life's inevitable antagonisms are settled through finding synthesis (a middle way). Yet this introduces new conflicts – hence that classic outsider feeling of being permanently embattled.
3. Such battles result in progress, making embattled people the world's thinkers and progressives. We're the people trying to tackle the inevitable antagonisms, even if the initial result is unhappiness.
4. Kierkegaard refutes Hegel's notion that environmental factors determine conflicts' outcomes. We have free will to make our own decisions, he states, and to generate our own outcomes.
5. Yet our free will engenders the 'dizziness of freedom', which can induce anxiety, dread and despair.
6. Nietzsche declares that 'God is dead', which means our higher values must come from within. We must take possession of our own thoughts – and seek truth.

7. He throws down the gauntlet: our destiny is to become the 'superman' – transcending our own limitations to be guided by our self-developed ideals and morals.

8. 'Existence precedes essence' contends Sartre, meaning that humans have no purpose other than to exist, which makes us free to develop our unique form. *Nothing* is ordained.

9. Yet 'with freedom comes responsibility'. We owe it to ourselves to both ask questions – especially of authority – and pursue answers, regardless of whether this makes us miserable. Happiness is not the point – truth is the point.

10. That said, our suffering ceases once it's given meaning, says Frankl. We must therefore discover the meaning within our pain – using our struggles as the lever for this vital discovery. It's this that will give us our *edge*.

The enlightenment of existentialism completes our self-examination, and with it the potential self-obsession of the outsider. From here on, it's all about the future. And it's also about facing out. It's about developing our potential and using our unique perspective to forge an edge.

PART TWO

The Rebel *with* a Cause

5

FINDING MEANING

'All the animals come out at night: whores, skunk pussies, buggers, queens, fairies, dopers, junkies. It's sick. Venal. Someday a real rain will come and wash all this scum off the streets.'

For movie portrayals of the outsider, few can beat Martin Scorsese's 1976 classic *Taxi Driver*. Failing to cope with his post-Vietnam stress, Travis Bickle (Robert De Niro) takes a job as a night-time New York cabbie. Yet, rather than cure his insomnia, his nocturnal ferrying of the city's low-life fuels his anger at the immoral cesspit beyond his window, hence the quote above as he contemplates a rainy night in a seedy Times Square.

A generation on from Holden Caulfield's forlorn wanderings and Manhattan's descended into a dystopian urban hell. It's the perfect setting for a young and idealistic drifter to charge up his moral indignation to breaking point. Like Caulfield, Travis seeks innocence and purity: first finding it in the well-educated Betsy (Cybill Shepherd). She eventually rejects his ill-mannered clumsiness, causing Bickle's attentions to turn towards the drug-addled teenage prostitute Iris (Jodie Foster), who becomes his cause, as well as his catalyst for action.

Travis himself is portrayed as an unstable itinerant. He's the loner in the crowd making others feel uncomfortable and the authorities watchful. Yet, essentially, he's mentally isolated and socially awkward: a classic outsider.

'Loneliness has followed me my whole life,' says Travis, echoing Nietzsche as he turns himself into a moral and physical übermensch. 'Everywhere: in bars, in cars, sidewalks, stores, everywhere. There's no escape. I'm God's lonely man.'

For all his extreme language and behaviour there's something of Travis in most outsiders. There certainly was in me. I almost envied his post-traumatic stress – justifying the anger that fuelled his courage, allowing him to make radical and decisive turns in his life. He didn't just complain about the 'scum' on the streets or the meaninglessness of his existence: he did something about it – caring little for the consequences.

Fearing failure within conformity

I had similar notions. Not of resorting to violence or vigilantism, I hasten to add, but of what I called my 'virtual suicide'. This would be the moment I'd turn my back on the suffocating imprisonment of normal adult pursuits. Like Travis, I saw myself as a night-time taxi driver. I longed to be the remote and anonymous figure in the front seat: the man exploring the absurdity of existence while chauffeuring party-goers and drunks around central London.

It would be a pointless pursuit, yet one absolving me of the need to 'get on' within orthodox careers that secretly terrified me. Particularly at night, taxi-driving felt like the occupational equivalent of staring out of the café window – searching for meaning while watching life at its most wretched.

I was fantasizing, of course. While I feared the negative consequences of career failure – to the point of mentally inventing an escape – I feared more the irreparable damage of such a leap. Instead, I stayed in what renowned life-coach Lindsey Agness calls the 'grey zone'. Here, we earn a living and even become financially comfortable, while remaining tremendously frustrated by our enforced conformity.

Yet the grey zone goes beyond career pursuits – taking us right back to Erik Erikson's identity-focused lifecycle struggles. Indeed, his developmental battles also covered adulthood:

From years 18–35 – and with our identity battles settled (or not) – Erikson's struggle is one of *intimacy* versus *isolation*. Here, we succeed or fail in forming loving relations – with outsiders clearly falling into the latter category, resulting in mental and potentially physical confinement (certainly Travis Bickle's predicament).

And from 35–64 we struggle between *generality* and *stagnation*. At this point, we're either making progress on all fronts – our life having both meaning and balance in areas such as family and career. Or we remain confused and frustrated, as well as self-absorbed, and with a nagging – or even overwhelming – sense of uselessness: something that can pervade all areas of our life.

The danger of downward mobility

It was the prospect of such stagnation – of being stuck in a meaningless grey zone – that drove my taxi driver fantasy: a negative or anti-ambition generated by the fear of having ambition and failing. Yet, in retrospect, it wasn't simply fear that kept me in the grey zone. It was my non-existent focus on the positive potential of my negativity. I had no idea what the upside looked like – except perhaps an ill-formed romantic notion of using my downward mobility for some Orwell-style reportage on London's nocturnal underworld.

Indeed, downward mobility is a common lifestyle choice for the outsider – not least because it's easy. Fearing failure (meaning the fear of trying but failing – resulting in humiliation), we feel more comfortable sliding down the scale than battling our way up. It looks radical, even cool. And, in my case, it reflected my unconscious negative self-beliefs.

Any attempt to escape the grey zone of conformity through downward mobility is certain to increase our frustration, however; at least once the immediate sense of liberation wears off. For the escape to be sustainable – for it to be a virtual rebirth rather than a virtual suicide – we must escape upwards, towards our greatest ambitions rather than down into the sewers that disguise our mental anguish. And this requires us to calculate a positive outcome for all the angst and aggravation we put ourselves through: something that gives us the required *edge* to succeed, on our own terms, as an outsider.

As Viktor Frankl implored, we must find meaning – especially from previous suffering. Only then can we start to calculate the positive potential from our outsider status. In fact, finding our *edge* works both ways: finding meaning is the key to gaining the *edge* required to succeed as an outsider, while gaining an *edge* (perhaps in something we excel) is the key to finding meaning. They are symbiotic endeavours.

And if Frankl can find meaning within the desperation of camp life – and use that to gain an *edge* through his positive contribution to the world's understanding of suffering – surely we can find meaning from our own anxieties, pain and experiences, as well as use that to develop our *edge*?

The personal notion of suffering

Of course, Frankl's search for meaning was clearly apparent given the extremity of his suffering, while his psychiatric training gave him the *edge* required to explore it. Meanwhile, being stuck in Agness's grey zone hardly counts by comparison. Yet that's to miss Frankl's point, which is that our notion of suffering is entirely personal. If we experience inner agony – perhaps through alienation, isolation, confusion, frustration or simply feeling misunderstood – we suffer, no matter how others judge the degree of suffering. We're the arbiter of our own suffering. So we can ignore the external admonishments of those suggesting we 'stop moaning' or 'get over it'.

And just as our suffering's personal, Frankl's notion of 'finding meaning' is also tailor-made. As a psychiatrist, he decided to combine his skills and experiences to explore the human condition. His suffering gave him clarity of purpose – yet a very personal purpose based on his unique insight. For our suffering to gain meaning, therefore – and for it to give us the required *edge* – it must have personal significance. It must be *our* meaning based on *our* insight.

This is a unique quest, but probably the most important exploration of our lives. What gives our suffering meaning? And how can that meaning develop into a positive purpose? That's the route to salvation for the outsider.

'What man actually needs is not some tensionless state but rather the striving and struggling for some goal worthy of him,' wrote Frankl. 'What he needs is not the discharge of tension at any cost, but the call of a potential meaning waiting to be fulfilled by him.'

That's how we forge an *edge* – by developing goals that turn our negative ambitions positive. It's such a goal that will start the process of removing the disadvantages from outsiders by giving them something to strive for – as well as the grit and will to succeed.

Finding our unique insight

So how do we find a goal or mission worthy of giving our suffering meaning? Not easy, though nothing is for the outsider. We can start by self-critically examining our particular anguish, and then by focusing on the insight this offers. From here, meaning, purpose and even a mission can be developed, although we must be aware that no neon light flashing the words 'here is your mission' will appear. As Frankl said, meaning is something we must discover and develop. It won't just happen.

Frankl's message chimes with those of cultural thinker Roman Krznaric. In his book *How to Find Fulfilling Work* (2012), Krznaric suggests that those with the most fulfilling lives do not have a job, or even a career. They have a vocation – something all outsiders should look for if their lives are to have meaning. Yet a vocation is something we must develop.

'I regularly hear people lament that they are "still searching for their vocation" or envying others who have "found their ultimate calling",' writes Krznaric. 'Their search, however, is almost certain to be unsuccessful. Not because vocations do not exist. But because we have to realize that a vocation is not something we *find*, it's something we *grow* – and grow into.'

For Krznaric, a vocation emerges from within what we already do. Just as Frankl's professional training led to his insights into human suffering – and even Travis Bickle's troubling mission to rid New York of the 'scum' developed from within his wayward career as a night-time cab-driver – so our vocation will emerge once we're on the right path, doing what we're meant to do. That said, Bickle is hardly a strong role-model for finding meaning – more an example of what can go wrong when we look in the wrong place.

Luckily, Krznaric offers a better example: Marie Curie. Born in Poland – the fifth and youngest child – to a family much-reduced in circumstances, Curie fought against intellectual snobbery and ingrained sexism to discover the properties of radioactivity, a world-changing feat eventually recognized through becoming the first female Nobel Prize winner.

Curie was undoubtedly a disadvantaged outsider. She had to battle against the frustrations of her circumstances, her immigrant status, the pretensions of late-nineteenth century Paris, and – especially – the gender prejudice of the age, which sometimes required her husband to make presentations of her work to scientific societies. Yet, through it all, she was undeterred – battling away in her laboratory (even on her wedding day) until her mission emerged.

She describes it thus:

'Life is not easy for any of us. But what of that? We must have perseverance and above all confidence in ourselves. We must believe we are gifted for something, and that this thing, at whatever cost, must be attained.'

Believing we're gifted for something

This is a key message for any outsider, although the actual substance of our gift may not – yet – be obvious. Meanwhile, it's important to note that both Curie's gift and vocation emerged through years of work and study – something Krznaric's keen to emphasize with respect to vocation.

'There is a widespread – and mistaken – assumption that a vocation usually comes to people in a flash of enlightenment or moment of epiphany,' he writes – also suggesting that an equally mistaken alternative is via a self-reflective process in which the answer miraculously appears at the bottom of the page.

Indeed, it's this expectation that frustrates so many outsiders – perhaps leading many to chop and change their careers and identities in their search for meaning (certainly my experience). For Krznaric, purpose emerges once we're heading in the right direction, which means – at this stage – our primary concern is the direction of travel.

It's how we set our compass that's critical. And it's that setting that should become the number one quest of any outsider searching for meaning.

Setting the compass

Certainly, the need is to set the compass positively. We must reject any notion of downward mobility or virtual suicide. That said, this is far easier than it seems. A simple mental exercise can turn our negative thinking positive. Ask adolescent outsiders what they want to do and many will look uncomfortable, shrug their shoulders and mumble 'I dunno'. Pressed, they may say 'I just wanna be me' or 'I wanna do my own thing'.

Of course, this is usually both expressed and received as a negative ambition. As a statement of refusal as well as a plea to 'back off'. Yet by reversing this negative trajectory we can quickly find a positive path forward. Lost souls (not just adolescents) pleading to be allowed to 'be themselves' are making a statement – not *against* conformity – but *for* non-conformity. They're asking for the discretion to explore their own interests and express themselves freely.

Quite right too, although this leads immediately to the next question: in what do you want to freely express yourself? What do you enjoy? Chances are, it's what you're good at. For me it was writing – at school, I enjoyed writing essays because I was good at them. Others may like art or music or IT or maths. So we can add to the earlier statement 'I want to express myself freely' by stating 'I want to express myself freely in English/maths/art etc.' – deleting or adding as appropriate. We now have a positive – if somewhat vague – direction for our pursuits without compromising our freedom of expression.

Next, we need to think about the positive avenues for our self-expression. In my case (with writing) there were many – including journalism, book-writing, copy-editing, script-writing, even poetry – as there are in all aspects of modern life.

In fact, even within these avenues there are many divisions or genres. For instance, book-writing brings with it the key split between fiction and non-fiction, with each of these dividing into myriad sectors and sub-sectors. Of course, each division narrows the options, which can feel like entrapment, although it shouldn't. It should feel like a step towards developing our own unique brand of non-conformity.

Overly critical parents, siblings and teachers

'But I'm rubbish at everything,' is a common response to this early plea for direction. This is, of course, a lie – though an understandable one based on the fears generated by low self-esteem and alienation. Yet we're all good at something. And it's on that *thing* we need to focus our energies, or on finding what that *thing* is if we've yet to discover it.

Too often it's poor conditioning, perhaps due to overly-critical parents, siblings or teachers, or due to the dreadful quality of our education – or all the above, as it sometimes seems in my case – that stops us from recognizing our positive attributes. And while this is a crime against us – one that should, indeed, make us angry – it at least offers the 'suffering' Frankl views as the necessary prerequisite for finding true meaning.

In fact, overcoming our poor conditioning, and/or our low-grade education, are excellent missions – and ones Frankl would no doubt judge highly worthwhile given the victory of ignorance and paranoia he was forced to endure. That said, such an internal mission, while worthy, will require an external purpose if it's to provide the meaning we seek or the *edge* we need. However tempting, it cannot be about 'self-discovery' alone – although that can form part of the mix.

10 signposts towards finding meaning

Finding meaning is not easy. It's not meant to be easy. Yet it's so important to our future well-being as outsiders that it requires thought and self-examination to a depth not plunged before. In fact, as Krznaric states, even this is unlikely to generate the instant, flashing, message of meaning we're expecting. That said, we can look for signposts along the way.

Here are some thoughts on finding them:

1. *Focus on the anguish.* The very thing that generates your pain may well be where you should look for salvation. Ultimately, mine focused on my appalling education – something I was determined to overcome (at least in the key areas that interested me) once its paucity became apparent.
2. *Make it a positive pursuit.* Yet, 'self-discovery' cannot form the entire solution. While sounding positive, such a focus is on removing past deficits rather than incrementally pursuing future attainment, which requires a tangible quest – usually something with a public outlet (see Chapter 6).
3. *Look in the right place.* My father insisted on introducing me to the building industry, a career I hated for its overly-macho

provincialism and precise calculations. Meanwhile, I loved the unruly urban intellectualism of the newspaper industry – so took a job selling small ads at *The Independent* to get myself through the right door. No matter that I was doing the wrong job, it was in the right place – and I could soon start calculating my move across to the editorial side (as I did by submitting articles for their youth section).

4. *What holds your attention?* We can be interested in many things, but a vocation requires us to home in on just one. This can be frustrating – not least because many outsiders are intellectual butterflies. So it's probably worth noting what holds your attention and seeing where that can take you. My best subjects were English and history, which generated an interest in politics that merged with my love of writing to suggest journalism as my (eventual) path.

5. *Ignore monetary concerns.* We need to eat, of course. But, especially when young, there's almost a romantic requirement for the outsider to financially struggle as they seek out their vocation. While poverty is not an essential requirement – being a tramp doesn't make you Orwell, after all – making decisions based on monetary concerns, at least at this stage, is a long way from finding meaning.

6. *Broaden your horizons.* Having too narrow an outlook can be crippling. This is often a geographical constraint. Certainly, the cultural and intellectual poverty of exurban Essex combined with the moral strictures of lower-middle class life to offer me little in the way of stimulation. Luckily, London was just 30 minutes down the line, which is where I moved aged 19, and I have loved big cities ever since.

7. *Open your mind.* Narrow horizons are not solely geographic. Attitude has a lot to do with it. If we assume we'll fail to find our vocation, then we'll almost certainly prove ourselves right. We'll find reasons to discount every option almost immediately. Yet seek and you shall find. So open your mind to what's possible.

8. *Discriminate.* Yet we can also go the other way – grabbing every half-opportunity in the belief that it offers salvation. I can remember meeting a London tour guide for rich Americans and thinking 'yes, yes: that's it!' Thank God he ignored my overly-enthusiastic responses or I'd have been led down yet another career cul-de-sac. Compromise is important but we need to be able to join the dots towards our preferred outcome – not clutch at different things in the hope something sticks.

9. *Do some research.* These days there's no need to grab opportunities based on happenstance. The Internet provides all the tools required to not only discover, but to research, assess and – if necessary – approach any avenue we think could work for us. Not that the Internet's everything. I won both my place at university and my first job in financial journalism from well-written letters to key people, having first phoned the institutions I favoured.

10. *Beware the saviour.* Open your mind to opportunities and others will spot the vacancy – not all of whom will have your best interests at heart. Of course, on occasion this can be the perfect union of needs and wants. But in your enthusiasm for finding the *thing*, you may ignore the fact that what's being offered isn't what it seems. Lost souls are often found by missionaries looking for recruits. Far better to develop your own goals and find your own recruits, than end up embittered by following the plans of someone who'd spotted your floundering goal-quests and deceived you into becoming a crewman for theirs.

6

THE PURSUIT OF EXCELLENCE

Finding meaning requires focus. It's that simple. Just as identity-hoppers fall, each time, to the bottom of any new hierarchy – a position outsiders inherently dislike – so our lack of sustained focus prevents us developing the *edge* required to find meaning (as well as the meaning required to forge that *edge*).

Of course, this poses an immediate dilemma. If we have to home in on that one *thing*, what should it be? We each have a single path towards salvation, goes the theory, so we have to find it. For some – perhaps talented musicians or artists – the pursuit's obvious. Yet for many others – and particularly for outsiders – it's a trickier concern, not least because our sense of isolation may originate from our failure to find any pursuit worthy of our singular attention.

One aspect of finding the true path seems obvious to me, however, so it's worth stating upfront. Outsiders that find meaning – and especially those affecting revolutionary change – are pursuing excellence in a particular area. We all excel at something, or can if given the tools and training. And it's here where we should focus our energies.

Only through achieving excellence will we dispel any doubts that we're on the right path – or at least reduce them given that, for disadvantaged outsiders, some doubt is inevitable. Only via excellence will we silence our detractors, real or imagined. And only through the pursuit of excellence will we gain the *edge* required to succeed in a world dominated by advantaged insiders.

That one *thing*

Finding that one thing can be an agonizing choice for many, not least because we may think we lack excellence: as well we might. Dire educational experiences or perhaps poor conditioning may have prevented us spotting, let alone pursuing, any nascent talent or aptitude in a particular field.

That said, our response to this should be one of anger. *How dare they write us off at such a young age!* And it should also be one of defiance. Searching and finding meaning is now an imperative – compelling us to prove them wrong. We owe it to ourselves to stick it to them in this respect: making seeking and accomplishing excellence a key part of our journey towards finding meaning, no matter what the agonies.

That said, any 'screw you'-style motivation – while initially powerful – is unlikely to see us through the inevitable setbacks such a journey entails. It can, in fact, make setbacks harder to overcome because, in the back of our minds, we'll be thinking 'perhaps they were right all along'. Perhaps we really weren't up to it after all.

What's needed is not blind fury and a desire for revenge but the right mindset for the pursuit of excellence. In this respect, a key requirement is to never view excellence as a destination: it's a journey – a direction of travel. There's no final arrival or moment in which we're 'full' when it comes to our skills or talents. Excellence is a continuous pursuit – a path that's followed no matter what bends and diversions appear along the way.

And if we start further back on the grid than others – due to poor conditioning or our deficient education, or (just as likely) our closed-minded attitude to learning – then so be it. Any acceleration through the ranks will feel that much more exhilarating.

Required: a growth mindset

Thinkers both new and old can help us adjust to the notion that, for outsiders, life's a journey rather than a destination. For the new, we should turn to Stanford University psychologist Carol Dweck. Her excellent 2006 book *Mindset* divides humanity into those with a *fixed mindset* and those with a *growth mindset*. This is an important distinction as those with a *fixed mindset* view their attributes as set, potentially from birth. They are as they are, and spend much of their time trying to either prove or communicate their worth or – more likely – trying to hide their self-perceived limitations.

'Believing that your qualities are carved in stone – *the fixed mindset* – creates an urgency to prove yourself over and over,' writes Dweck. 'If you have only a certain amount of intelligence, a certain personality, a certain moral character – well, you'd better prove that you have a healthy dose of them. It simply wouldn't do to look or feel deficient in these most basic characteristics.'

Those with a *growth mindset*, meanwhile, assume they've everything to learn, and that all encounters can feed their appetite for mental growth – helping them continuously sharpen their skills and knowledge (indeed, their *edge*).

'This *growth mindset* is based on the belief that your basic qualities are things you can cultivate through your efforts,' writes Dweck. 'Although people may differ in every which way – in their initial talents and aptitudes, interests, or temperaments – everyone can change and grow through application and experience.'

On meeting people, the instincts of those with a *growth mindset* is not 'how can I impress this person?' but 'what can this person teach me?' – a far more enabling attitude. If you have a *fixed mindset* you're trying to convince others (and yourself) you 'have a royal flush when you're secretly worried it's a pair of tens,' says Dweck. For those with a *growth mindset*, meanwhile, 'the hand you're dealt [is] just the starting point for development'.

Certainly, it's depressing to conclude we've spent our life trapped within a *fixed mindset* – perhaps due to an understandable defensiveness triggered by overly-critical elders or poor childhood conditioning. Yet let's commute the life sentence for a moment. We can also realize that – if having a *fixed mindset* is what's blocking our route towards both excellence and, from that, finding meaning – it's little more than an instant flick of our mental switch to adopt a *growth mindset*. We simply need to open our mind to growth, rather than spend our time attempting to prove our fixed attributes.

In this respect, Dweck's insight is a liberating revelation – one offering us the key to mental freedom by so perfectly describing the cage within which we think. We're trapped within a negative, defensive mentality. And this adds to our disadvantages, blunting our *edge*. So let's change direction through the application of a new, development-oriented, *edge*-sharpening, way of thinking.

Of course, it's not that easy. A *fixed mindset* is an ingrained trait that requires constant vigilance to overcome. Yet we now have sight of the beast, which makes it easier to slay. In fact, Dweck's given us the weapons to kill it, even if we'll have to kill it again tomorrow – and the next day.

Aristotle's pursuit of the 'good life'

As for the old thinker: that's Aristotle – the father of western rational thought and a huge influence on modern science, ethics, psychology, biology, politics and literature. In fact, Aristotle even qualifies as an outsider. Born in the unfashionable Greek province of Thrace in 384BC, his parents died while he was a child – resulting in him being sent to Athens to be educated. He wound up in Plato's Academy where he prospered despite being viewed as a brainy though moody provincial, and certainly not one of the inner clique.

Overlooked as Plato's successor at the Academy in favour of an Athenian, Aristotle (somewhat piqued) left Athens only to return aged 50 to set up his own school: the Lyceum. Here, Aristotle's pupils discussed life's weightier questions while standing in a public walkway, hence them becoming known as the Peripatetics (the 'walkers') – an outsider label if ever there was one.

As for Aristotle's philosophy, well how's this for an existentialist quote to rival Nietzsche and Sartre: 'Man is a goal-seeking animal. His life only has meaning if he is reaching out and striving for his goals.'

For Aristotle, thinkers divide into those with goals, who are motivated to plan and act, and those without – who'll spend much of their time staring out of café windows pondering existential dilemmas. What's more, if mental well-being is the desired end-result, then desires such as health or wealth are no more than resources helping us gain the *edge* required for achieving our higher goals. This is the *ergon* ('function' or 'task') of human living.

The human soul is a connected series of capacities, says Aristotle. The nutritive soul is responsible for growth and reproduction, in common with all living things. The perceptive soul is for motion and sensory perception, in common with animals. And the rational soul is for intellectual reasoning – a capacity peculiar to humans. And it's our scope for rationality that guides us towards a potentially better life, claims Aristotle.

So we must reason well in order to live a fulfilled life: the 'good life' as he termed it. And, for Aristotle, living well means *doing something*, not just being in a certain state or condition but teleologically sourcing goals involving the attainment of virtue via excellence – both attributes defined and motivated by the rational soul. Being mentally in a good place is not enough. We must achieve something to the absolute best of our abilities, even if we've yet to establish what those best abilities consist of.

Excellence within a community

Yet there's an interesting rider to Aristotle's thinking with respect to attaining virtue through goal pursuits and excellence. As stated, he considered health and wealth resources for the attainment of higher goals. They're not goals in themselves. Nonetheless, he was clear that those lacking an adequate supply of 'other goods' (as he called them) would most likely fall short in their quest.

He goes beyond health and wealth in this respect. If we are friendless, childless, powerless, weak and/or ugly, our opportunities for achieving excellence will be limited. Fulfilment, for Aristotle, requires good fortune in all these areas. So we must be minded that – while focusing on excellence – balance is required.

Certain elements – such as the need for children – can be viewed as the values of his day rather than universal laws. Meanwhile, strength can be expanded to include mental fortitude and beauty can be interpreted as physical or mental fitness. Yet Aristotle's message tells us that a rounded vision of fulfilment is required. For outsiders, this can also, and crucially, be interpreted as the need for achieving excellence within a community. Whatever we do *must* have a public outlet. Achievement in isolation will simply reinforce our alienation. It's excellence without virtue, which will push us further into the wilderness.

Of course, we can define our own community and even create one – perhaps our associates and peers in our own version of Aristotle's Lyceum. Eventually, however, external recognition will be an important confirmation of our having, indeed, found both excellence and meaning, and of having forged our *edge*.

Given outsiders' propensity for isolation, this is an important point. Excellence in something that has only personal value – such as computer games or train set modelling – lacks public virtue and therefore reinforces, rather than positively directs, our alienation. That said, exhibiting model railways at public fairs is fantastically meaningful, not least because there's a community of modellers highly-focused on excellence, innovation and external acknowledgement.

What should we do with our lives?

But we've still not answered the crucial question: what should we do? Indeed, the direction of our pursuit – especially if requiring both focus and balance, as well as excellence – remains the great imponderable, and is ultimately a very personal decision. It can also take several goes.

Po Bronson's thoughtful 2003 book *What Should I Do With My Life?* can perhaps shed light on such dilemmas. The book is the 'true story of people who answered the ultimate question' – narrated by a man that threw in a career as a bond salesmen to become the chronicler (for *Wired* magazine and others) of the burgeoning 1990s Silicon Valley of his adopted San Francisco Bay area. Finding himself at a career crossroads, Bronson decided to look for guidance and courage from others that had 'unearthed their true calling'. 'Those who broke away from the chorus to learn the sound of their own voice,' as Bronson elegantly puts it.

In each of the 50 or so case studies – from young and old, disadvantaged and advantaged, local or global – Bronson describes messy and complicated modern lives: the antithesis of the happily-ever-after predestination that peppers many of the 'how I made it' biographies of the famous. To outsiders, the book reads like a compendium of fellow strugglers – for the most part finding, or at least groping towards, an answer.

There's always something nagging away at our conscience, suggests Bronson. Something that says, if I could do anything, *this* would be it. It's an incessant voice, though one we *must* listen to. Of course, we need to rationalize it by calculating how we can turn such dreams into a practical path – perhaps with milestones along the way. But it's a voice that won't go away, and nor should it.

Yet there's no comforting 'cure-all' he concludes, though most of his interviewees possess a deep integrity, a higher calling and a desire to 'make a difference' – many via entrepreneurialism in one form or another (see Chapter 7). Nonetheless, Bronson makes it abundantly clear from the outset: 'It's not easy/It's not *supposed* to be easy/Most people make mistakes/Most people have to learn the hardest lessons more than once.'

'Don't look for a story just like yours,' he concludes. 'There is no story just like yours. Open up your filter and you will recognize that all stories are unique and all stories are worthy. Your story is unique. Find your story.'

The key need: be incremental

No doubt Bronson's mention of deep integrity will have generated a reaction from many outsiders, renowned as we are for our 'highly-individualistic' moral compass. Yet this isn't an insistence on becoming a tree-hugging do-gooder. In fact, it's the opposite. This is about you pursuing *your* goals to help satisfy *your* calling. Make no mistake, it's a selfish act. That said, it's clear to me that Bronson's interviewees seem most settled – and most motivated – once they're in some respects making a positive difference.

Many of Bronson's interviewees go on to pursue highly-profitable enterprises – some having rejected lucrative mainstream careers. Others have rejected dead-end jobs to do something more philanthropic. Some spurn big things for small, while others swap small things for big. Each time, however, they're moving towards something that inspires them into becoming their best selves. And this usually involves adding positively to their chosen field: whether through innovation, by pushing the boundaries of their art, or by 'giving back' in some way or other.

In short, they're being incremental – adding to the sum spirit of the world in some way, which I think is a vital need when both finding meaning and forging an *edge*, even if our motives for doing so are selfish.

From Little Acorns

So are there any rules for finding our *thing*? From reading Krznaric, Dweck, Bronson and many others – and from my own experiences and observations – I think the following is a reasonable guide (no more) if struggling to find that little acorn.

1. *It will be an acorn.* No great oak will present itself, so we must find the right acorn. Of course, there are lots of acorns, so picking *the one* can be tricky. As Bronson says, 'Usually, all we

get is a glimmer. A story we read or someone we briefly met. A curiosity. A meek voice inside, whispering. It's up to us to hammer out the rest.'

2. *Look for excellence.* The pursuit of excellence is a key need for any outsider, especially those wishing to reject some seemingly predetermined path. So the acorn to pick is the one giving us the best hope of achieving excellence. Certainly, linguists pursuing goals involving mathematics will increase their doubts regarding what's achievable beyond the mediocre, making failure more likely.

3. *It's unlikely to be your first acorn.* Just about every outsider story I've ever read or heard involves some form of change of direction, if not several. My father assumed my destiny was in the building industry: a non-future I spent four years pursuing through work and college before realizing it just wasn't me – despite being told many times it was my only chance for professional attainment.

4. *Pursue what excites.* We tend to enjoy things we're good at and what we're good at tends to excite us. Yet we could be good at a range of things, so we must therefore look for excitement. What makes the pulse quicken, the pace accelerate and the hairs on our arms stand up? That's what we'll return to again and again, so that's where we belong.

5. *Expect to struggle.* Innate talent is a myth. Excellence only comes to those that struggle. Of course, the struggle's not the point. We're not here to be miserable or stressed or tired. But at least then we know we're pushing ourselves through the inevitable 'wilderness years' before our excellence is recognized (though we must never think ourselves 'full' in terms of talent).

6. *Avoid wasteful hedonism.* Lost and especially disadvantaged outsiders often pursue hedonistic goals as a way of numbing the pain or denying their anger. This is, of course, wasteful – as I know from my own party-going indulgences during low points in my career. Yet, even here, a *growth mindset* can open our eyes to the opportunities. I have friends that are now successful DJs, while

others are nightclub promoters – including one on behalf of an innovative charity – and another who started a magazine for dance music DJs: all from pursuing their love of nightlife.

7. *Avoid shallow objectives.* This is not a call for worthy pursuits. Yet if our goals are shallow they won't motivate us and we're more likely to fail. If we want to be 'rich' or 'famous' then we're, in fact, not pursuing goals at all: we're trying to overcome our insecurities about being poor and/or unknown. In fact, the pursuit of wealth or celebrity for its own sake will only exacerbate our insecurities, because there will always be someone richer or more famous.

8. *Think long term.* Many people fail after achieving their short-term goals because they've not considered 'what's next?' Far better to pursue a longer timeframe – perhaps 10 years – which gives us enough time to not only find our higher calling but to acquire the required skills as well as make significant headway. It may not be enough to turn our acorn into a majestic oak. But it's certainly long enough to see the future tree in prospect.

9. *It's the direction that matters.* Sorry to switch metaphors but, if the timeframe's 10 years, the destination may be no more than a hazy shape in the distance. Fine: establishing the destination is only vital for setting the compass and calculating some milestones along the way (that confirm the direction). And such well-directed endeavours should not only continually excite us – giving us that feeling of arrival as we reach each milestone – they'll improve our judgement as decisions are a lot easier when assessing what supports our journey, and what doesn't.

10. *Innovate.* And, finally, there's the hallmark of the successful outsider – what sets apart the Bowies, the Emins and the Edisons from the rest of the pack. We must innovate. Excellence isn't enough. What's important is using that talent to change things. This doesn't have to be huge, but it has to be significant enough to be self-confirming. In any pursuit, there's the next – undiscovered – level. *Make that your discovery.* Indeed, that's why the destination's hazy: you've yet to invent it.

7

THE ENTREPRENEURIAL SPIRIT

So *excellence* builds our path towards *meaning* by giving us an edge. Knowing this is a great first step. But how do we proceed? And how do we maintain progress through what can seem like a dense thicket of false starts, setbacks and seemingly insurmountable barriers?

We become an entrepreneur, that's how. Don't worry, this isn't a treatise to starting a business: or, at least, not just starting a business. It's about bundling the outsider's previously-disabling attributes and turning them into an unstoppable force for achievement. The entrepreneurial spirit is not only enabling, it's curative: forcing us to adopt a *growth mindset* as well as giving us the required drive to plan and achieve our goals – all while remaining uncompromisingly beyond the clan.

When it comes to sharpening our *edge*, nothing is so incisive as the entrepreneurial spirit.

What is an entrepreneur?

The dictionary definition of an entrepreneur – of 'someone organizing and managing an enterprise' – is clearly inadequate. Yet so is the modern image of jeans 'n' sneakers Silicon Valley types inventing apps and gizmos for smartphones and tablets. That said, such an image certainly works at one level: they're innovators.

In fact, go back to the nineteenth century and entrepreneurs were the mill or yard owners using new machinery to drive the industrial revolution in cities such as Manchester, Glasgow, Pittsburgh and Dortmund. Go back a little further, and entrepreneurs were the merchants establishing global trade – developing innovative concepts such as banking and insurance in ports such as London, Amsterdam and New York.

Each era, it seems, provides opportunities for buccaneering entrepreneurship for those removed from the established economy. Indeed, it's often cited that the British Empire prospered due to aristocratic primogenital inheritance rules. Under such rules, the younger sons (and all daughters) inherited nothing – resulting in hundreds of well-educated and well-connected people being forced to make a living from beyond their family estates. It was the opposite to pre-revolutionary France, where a bloated and unproductive aristocracy grew ever weaker by dividing inheritances between all the siblings – resulting in their eventual overthrow.

In nearly all cases, groups excluded from the mainstream economy make excellent entrepreneurs. A far higher percentage of immigrants become entrepreneurs in countries such as the US, Britain, Singapore and Australia than those born and bred in such countries. Meanwhile women (especially young mums) are the fastest-growing entrepreneurial cohort in many western economies – many citing exclusion, disillusionment or the inflexibility of traditional employment as their triggers for starting an enterprise. Others are simply contrarian – pursuing activities that go against the grain or bust convention, because that's how they view the world.

Of course, such a trait also makes them hard to define, as Daniel Isenberg discovered in *Worthless, Impossible and Stupid* (2013) – his highly-readable exploration of the entrepreneurial mind.

'The phenomenon of entrepreneurship is about contradicting our expectations, and so codification of the right or better or best way to be an entrepreneur will always possess an elusive quality,' writes Isenberg. 'The instant that we think we have it, the entrepreneur's job is to prove us wrong. The potentially extraordinary value resides precisely in showing how violating (or simply ignoring) the common prescriptions can work, sometimes amazingly well.'

So far, so outsider.

A selfish enterprise

An important point about entrepreneurship, however – at least for our purposes – is that entrepreneurs are innovators *for profit*. Their aim is to personally prosper from what they do. This removes people such as World Wide Web inventor Tim Berners-Lee – the privately-educated son of a computer scientist. He not only developed his invention within organizations such as the research facility at CERN, he never saw his work as a route towards personal gain. He just wasn't selfish enough. Ultimately, entrepreneurs are singularly obsessed with self-advancement, which doesn't preclude them from providing a public good: as long as it's wrapped within their personal goals.

Of course, entrepreneurship doesn't just mean business. Far from it. Take Damien Hirst: a modern artist worth a reputed £215 million (US$350 million). His father – a motor mechanic – abandoned his family while Damien was a child, turning Hirst into the rebellious schoolboy that scraped a place at the prestigious Goldsmiths College in London. While there, he organized art exhibitions in disused warehouses, as well as developing an eye for outrageous but bankable art. Notoriety and profitability have always gone hand-in-hand for Hirst, a combination that makes him both Britain's best-known, and richest, living artist – as well as a definite outsider.

Then there's J.K. Rowling, creator of the *Harry Potter* brand. Escaping from an 'abusive' marriage, 'Jo' became a clinically-depressed single parent living on state benefits in Edinburgh. Inspired by a mundane train journey to imagine a boy leaving for wizardry school, she became determined to complete the novel in her head despite her mental chaos – furiously writing chapters in cafés while her daughter slept in a buggy beside her. Seven books and eight films later, the brand is worth over £10 billion – largely thanks to Rowling's innovation, drive and furious focus on excellence.

What entrepreneurs are not

So the plea is to apply our potentially-innate entrepreneurial spirit, no matter what the pursuit. This involves working for ourselves rather than big organizations, being focused, being innovative and – importantly – seeking personal gain. Why is personal gain so important? Because that way lies sustainability. And only through sustainability will the disadvantaged outsider find meaning.

Yet there are also some entrepreneurial myths to explode, as Isenberg explains. Interestingly, he starts by exploding 'myth #1' – that 'entrepreneurs must be innovators'. By this he means that entrepreneurs do not need a 'wall of patents' or to somehow reinvent the wheel. He states that as much value is created not from revolutionary ideas, but from exploring gaps in existing markets.

This can be in any field – for instance, there was clearly a gap in the market for books about a boy wizard, as well as art made from dead animals. And it can be created from what Isenberg terms 'minnovation'. This is no more than an unexpected twist on an existing idea: 'the incessant counterintuitive tweaks of the business model, the minor product adaptation' that nonetheless establishes our offering as somehow unique.

Isenberg cites Cinemex, a start-up company that brought the 'old hat' concept of multiscreen cinemas to a huge new audience: Mexico.

'The only innovation we introduced was putting lime juice and chilli sauce on the popcorn instead of butter,' was how the founder Miguel Davila described it – overlooking the fact multiscreen cinemas in Mexico are a highly-innovative concept.

'When I speak to potential entrepreneurs,' says Davila (quoted by Isenberg), 'I tell them, don't expect that the sky's going to open and a lightning bolt is going to hit you with the next Facebook idea. Those things are Halley's comet – they come by once every hundred years.

You don't need to have that as an entrepreneur. You just have to figure out something people need [or may want] and find a way to execute it better than everyone else.'

Most renowned entrepreneurs agree with this.

'It really does not matter who gave birth to any particular idea,' writes publishing magnate, and definite outsider, Felix Dennis (1947–2014) in his frank and semi-biographical *How to Get Rich* (2006). 'This is borne out by the laws relating to patents and inventions. You cannot patent an idea. You can only patent your own method for implementing an idea. It is for this reason so many people have become rich despite never having had a single great idea in their lives. As it happens, I count myself among them.'

Excellence doesn't mean expertise

Isenberg's 'myth#2' is that 'entrepreneurs must be experts'. Oh dear, he now appears to be attacking the concept of excellence, although – again – all's not what it seems. This is not a plea for ignorance or poor execution: far from it. What he's saying is that a 'prior experience in the subject matter is certainly not a prerequisite, even for highly technical endeavours'.

'The real disruptors will be those individuals who are not steeped in one industry of choice,' says entrepreneur and prize-giver for entrepreneurial excellence Naveen Jain (quoted by Isenberg), 'but instead, individuals who approach challenges with a clean lens, bringing together diverse experiences, knowledge and opportunities . . . non-expert individuals will drive disruptive innovation.'

Far from an attack on expertise, Isenberg's view is that entrepreneurs often approach subjects from 'outside the box' – certainly a viewpoint likely to encourage innovative and contrarian ideas. And it's yet another endorsement for the outsider: our unique viewpoint being crucial for developing breakthrough, or at least incremental, innovations.

My own entrepreneurial experience may be instructive at this point. While a journalist, I noticed that – in the area of finance I covered – the public-relations offering was poor. As the unsexy end of financial services, the agency junior was usually assigned to the task of 'selling in' (persuading publications that their story was worth writing about). Yet they knew little of the complexities, thus irritating rather than persuading this grizzled editor.

And my frustrations were compounded once I became a banker, in what the City calls a 'gamekeeper turned poacher' move. The inhouse PR team was excellent, but 95 per cent focused on high-level fire-fighting, which meant it became my job, as the former hack, to source publicity for our departments' highly-innovative deals and concepts.

In fact, I was better at this than banking so found myself, at the age of 38, starting a PR agency specializing in corporate banking and finance. I lacked any expertise in how to offer agency-based PR although had a strong insight into how it should and shouldn't be done for my sector. Indeed, my agency – Moorgate Communications – remains an innovator for communicating complex ideas to sophisticated audiences: that's its USP (unique selling point) – something all entrepreneurial outsiders should develop.

Not so youthful

Isenberg's 'myth#3' is that 'entrepreneurs must be young'. Certainly, the emphasis on youth pervades all areas of creativity: 'young writer', 'young musician', 'young artist', 'young entrepreneur'. Once beyond our first flush of youth, it seems, the message is 'don't bother'. Powerful stereotypes support this notion: Bill Gates (Microsoft), Steve Jobs (Apple) and Mark Zuckerberg (Facebook) were all successful, and youthful, entrepreneurs, while Damien Hirst was the founder of an artistic group tagged the Young British Artists (the 'YBAs').

Yet, despite the noise, the evidence doesn't support the stereotype. A 2008 study of American entrepreneurs by researcher Vivek Wadhwa found double the number of founders over 50 as under 25, and that the average age for striking out alone was 40 for men and 41 for women. In fact, the highest cohort was the 55–64 age group.

Our obsession with youth seems to be part of the modern zeitgeist – perhaps the result of the sheer volume of innovation in the second half of the twentieth century, as well as the post-war demographic bulge (the 'baby-boomers') in the West, that started making a cultural impact from the 1960s onwards. Interestingly, Isenberg notes that the definition of 'young' seems to have crept up as this 'evergreen' generation has aged – with anyone below 50 now considered 'young' by many measures, when the cut-off was previously 25.

So we must also celebrate the creativity of older entrepreneurs in business and the arts. People like Canadian Roy Herbert Thomson (1894–1976). The son on an immigrant barber, Thomson failed as a farmer before returning to his ancestral Scotland to buy the ailing *Scotsman* newspaper aged 59. At the age of 63 he started Scottish Television and went on to buy *The Times* of London aged 70 (his name lives on in the Thomson Reuters multimedia corporation). Meanwhile, school dropout and step-father detester Colonel Harland David Sanders (1890–1980) opened his first Kentucky Fried Chicken outlet aged 65, and Ray Kroc (1902–1984) spent 17 years as an unknown musician and itinerant salesman before – while selling milkshake mixers – spotting the roll-out potential of McDonalds (then a single-site customer) aged 52.

Even in the arts, late developers make an impact. Alfred Hitchcock – the son of an Essex greengrocer – directed *Psycho* aged 61, while Picasso, Tolstoy, Goethe, Da Vinci and many others were producing some of their most critically-acclaimed work in their eighties.

Timing matters? Probably not

Isenberg expresses a fourth potential myth: that timing's everything. This myth states that it's not having the right product or even right vision that counts – nor the right approach. It's simply getting it on the table at the right moment. For instance, while many geeks were developing computer operating systems in the 1970s, Bill Gates succeeded because he pitched IBM at exactly the right moment. More recently, Google's Sergey Brin and Larry Page launched their page-ranking search engine just as the first wave of search-engine development was proving inefficient.

Yet Microsoft was launched in the teeth of the 1980 worldwide recession, while Google went commercial in 2000, just as the dotcom crash was tainting the entire sector – both inauspicious moments for launching corner-turning technologies within rapidly-developing sectors.

Many disruptive companies are launched in such circumstances – half the *Fortune 500* of leading US companies, according to Isenberg. Some reasons for this are obvious. The availability and price of assets (people, premises, machinery, etc.) is advantageous. Also, unemployment can force people to finally explore their long-suppressed venturing ideas – just as being a single mother on benefits led Rowling to write-up her wizarding fantasies. Yet there's also the stubbornness of the entrepreneur – someone that pursues a course simply because others are cautioning against it.

'There is a surprisingly ubiquitous relationship between adversity and entrepreneurship,' claims Isenberg. 'The overarching reason is that the process of entrepreneurship is seeing value where no one else does and persistently refusing to cave to the naysayers. This means that entrepreneurs are always bucking the current, going against fashion, doing what the rest of us think is not worth doing.'

Such gainsaying doesn't make the entrepreneurial leap easy. And the most rebellious outsiders can fear the consequences of launching into the unknown, even if it suits our notion of 'virtual suicide'. Indeed – particularly if they are a disadvantaged outsider – many close associates will have advised against it, which is perhaps why entrepreneurs of all stripes often cluster together in incubator-type buildings.

Of course, incubators (or artists' studios) can simply disguise the problem that entrepreneurship is often a highly-isolating experience.

Outsiders together – potentially all on the wrong path – can exacerbate rather than relieve the issues in the end, hence the need to seek some form of public acknowledgement for our venture: whether art, writing, music or business.

It doesn't have to be immediate. But, ultimately, artists must exhibit, writers publish and musicians perform. Meanwhile, businesses have to find customers. Otherwise, we're not entrepreneurs at all. We're isolationists, cutting ourselves off, which is self-defeating even if tempting when faced with others' disapproval.

Positives to entrepreneurship

Yet there are many positives to adopting entrepreneurialism as our route towards finding meaning. Renowned serial entrepreneur Luke Johnson – writing in his 2007 book *The Maverick* – offered 50 'reasons to become an entrepreneur'. They nearly all work for outsiders, but here are 10 particularly apt reasons (with some added thoughts of my own).

1. 'Because building your own company is the best fun you can have with your clothes on.' Entrepreneurship certainly suits the thrill-seeking adventurism of many outsiders, although can equally trigger our fears. Boring it ain't.
2. 'Because working for yourself is not just about becoming rich. It's about making things happen and making a difference,' which complements the outsider's need for finding meaning, as well as proves entrepreneurship is not just about business.
3. 'Because if you work for yourself you control your destiny.' Indeed, it's the loss of control that so often disturbs outsiders within formalized workplaces. In fact, if one word could sum up the positives of entrepreneurialism, it's 'autonomy'.
4. 'Because being an entrepreneur can be a highly creative endeavour' – again complementing the outsider's need for self-expression.

5. 'Because nothing beats overcoming the sceptics and making a new venture a roaring success.' A 'screw you' mentality can certainly get you going – although (as discussed) it's not a sustainable long-term driver.
6. 'Because you can explore your dreams in a way that's impossible to do as an employee' – or, indeed, as a dreamer.
7. 'Because when you meet other entrepreneurs you'll talk to them as equals.' This is an important need for outsiders, many of whom detest hierarchies, especially when at the bottom.
8. 'Because lots of successful entrepreneurs started with no qualifications or capital and still made it big – so why not you?' Certainly, the barriers to entry are low and becoming lower, no matter what the field.
9. 'Because the competition out there isn't really that good and you know you can do better.' This is a good starting point for any venture – a healthy disregard for your rivals, though one based on knowledge rather than arrogance.
10. 'Because life is not about excuses – it's about seizing the day.' *Carpe diem* indeed.

And in a later *Financial Times* column, Johnson offers his most eloquent reason for encouraging outsiders towards entrepreneurship.

'Possibly the best thing about working for oneself is that you don't have to do any arse-kissing,' he writes.

Actually, this isn't strictly true. As an entrepreneur I spend most of my time having to be nice to clients, potential clients, employees, potential employees, the bank manager, the landlord, key suppliers, etc. But, as Johnson says, 'generally speaking, the self-employed are required to tolerate and dispense considerably less insincere bullsh*t than is the norm within big organizations'.

Avoiding insincerity is a key driver for many entrepreneurs, just as it is for outsiders – taking us right back to Holden Caulfield's detestation of artificiality. Meanwhile the 'bullsh*t', as Johnson puts it, is a key reason many outsiders take one look at corporate life and run in the opposite direction.

Distilling the spirit

Yet have we fully-distilled the entrepreneurial spirit? Well, it doesn't come in a bottle – meaning there are some highly-individualistic qualities. And it's often wrongly-defined as a swashbuckling, devil-may-care attitude personified by the 'screw it let's do it' mantra of Richard Branson.

Of course, it does involve courage, though not bravado, and determination, though not inflexibility. Yet it's also highly practical. More than anything, I think it involves an eye for the main chance – or even the half-chance. It's a route towards gaining an *edge* by converting ideas into sustainable, hopefully profitable, ventures that have an impact, often via novelty, or at least through being incremental.

As for the mentality, I think Johnson gets close in *The Maverick*. In one passage he offers a checklist of differences between a corporate executive and an entrepreneur that reads like a psychometric test for insiders versus outsiders.

Here's just a flavour:

- [The executive] cares deeply about their CV, versus [the entrepreneur] doesn't have a CV.
- [Exec.] good at office politics, versus [entrep.] crap at office politics.
- Part of the establishment, versus anti-establishment.
- Lots of grand qualifications, versus hated school.
- Eminently employable, versus utterly unemployable.
- Highly clubbable, versus not very clubbable.
- Obsessed with status, versus obsessed with cashflow.
- Huge corner office, versus most practical low-cost office.
- First class travel, versus taking the bus if it makes sense.
- Membership of the poshest clubs, versus 70-hour weeks.
- Hierarchical structure, versus no structure.
- Risk-averse, versus opportunistic.

Of course, there are negative attributes to confess. Entrepreneurs are self-absorbed, socially awkward, contrary, individualistic and motivated by acclaim, though not necessarily by money and status. Yet these are balanced by the positives – including the fact entrepreneurs are driven, resilient, focused and practical.

Overall, and given all that entrepreneurship can offer outsiders, it's most definitely in our interest to develop the entrepreneurial spirit: taking heart from the fact entrepreneurs often succeed – and often make a difference – despite themselves.

Clearly outsiders should adopt an entrepreneurial attitude. Yet we still have to navigate the genuine disadvantages of being an outsider. To find meaning, and to forge an edge, we must develop the positive skills and attributes that can turn the disadvantaged outsider into one with strong advantages. This is our critical mission for Part Three.

PART THREE
Edge Ahead

8
DEVELOPING OUR CREATIVITY

'Enclosed in my own four walls, I found myself as an immigrant imprisoned in a foreign country . . . I saw my family as strange aliens whose foreign customs, rites and very language defied comprehension . . . though I did not want it, they forced me to participate in their bizarre rituals.'

Franz Kafka (1883–1924) was born to German-speaking Jewish parents in Prague – at the time a Czech-speaking outpost of the Austro-Hungarian Empire. His parents were ambitious fancy-goods retailers and rather proud of their status within both the Jewish community and the upper echelons of Prague society. The young Kafka, meanwhile, felt alienated from both his parents' heritage – as the diary entry above attests – and by his minority status.

Kafka was shy, as was his mother. He put this down to his father's authoritarian dominance, even psychological brutality, which resulted in a troubled relationship that deeply affected Franz throughout his short life. In his thirties, Kafka attempted to rationalize the relationship by writing his father a 50-page letter. Yet it degenerated into accusations of emotional abuse and hypocritical behaviour – a familiar trajectory for outsiders trying to tackle past pain.

Perhaps typically, the letter was never delivered. It came to public attention posthumously, as did much of Kafka's writing, including his best-known works *Der Process* (*The Trial*), *Der Schloss* (*The*

Castle) and *Amerika* – published respectively in 1925, 1926 and 1927. All three books required completion by his friend Max Brod, who'd inherited Kafka's variously-disorganized manuscripts with the instructions to burn them unread – an instruction Brod thankfully disobeyed.

Nonetheless, the instruction reveals a crucial point about Kafka. Such was his inner turmoil, one of the twentieth century's most celebrated outsiders knew nothing of the acclaim he attracted. He died unknown, with our knowledge of his work down to Brod – himself a prolific writer and lifelong supporter of his deeply-insecure college buddy.

For Kafka, life was a waste: lost too soon – he died aged 41 from complications brought on by tuberculosis – with his creativity almost entirely undiscovered. Sure, some short stories had been published in periodicals, including *The Metamorphosis* (1915). But his frustration – his sense of inferiority and his alienation from what he saw as a confusing, elitist and bureaucratic society – remained utterly unresolved: a classic and regrettable fate for disadvantaged outsiders.

An outsider looking out

Yet Kafka also offers some positive lessons for outsiders. While largely unsuccessful during his lifetime, he never surrendered his extraordinary creativity – absorbing himself in writing as his medium for expressing his inner turmoil and alienation. And the way he contemplated this personal darkness is also worthy of attention. Despite spending much of his life lonely, depressed and even occasionally suicidal, Kafka's best works acted as a fantastical lens on the world rather than as a platform for philosophical navel-gazing or self-aggrandizement.

His best works – *The Trial* and *The Castle* – were an outsider's perspective on the authoritarian undercurrents that dominated Austro-Hungarian life. They were imaginative, satirical criticisms of turn-of-the-century European social structures that – ultimately – found a far wider audience than the often self-obsessed writings of the existentialists (who nonetheless claim Kafka as one of their own). Certainly, Kafka's claustrophobia comes through – reflecting his sense of rejection as well as his deep frustration at an inner creativity that had to take second place to what he called his *brotberuf* (bread job).

This was as a clerk at the *Workers' Accident Insurance Institute.* He hated it, although it inspired him to explore his repressed anarchic tendencies in his writings. His characters were often ordinary people battling faceless but impenetrable impediments. Yet the *brotberuf* restricted his time for creativity: endeavours that were further weakened by what would now be diagnosed as a rampant sex/porn addiction – a wasteful, all-consuming habit for a lonely and alienated young man.

Given this, Kafka acts as both an inspiration and a warning to outsiders seeking redemption by exploring their creativity. He's immortalized in his native Prague – celebrated as a writer and thinker more deeply than Paris hails Sartre. Yet he died alone in a sanatorium, his genius unheralded beyond the small Prague writers' circle centred around Brod. A clique, what's more, that only succeeded in triggering Kafka's imposter convictions.

The creative *edge*

Kafka's creativity gave his life meaning. But he lacked the *edge* required to make it profitable in his own lifetime. He assumed his talents worthless, as – without Brod – they would have been: hence the warning for outsiders. Make no mistake, accolades – including statues, guided tours and even adjectives – are useless to a dead outsider. Our creativity must count while we're alive and able to profit from its impact – something we can only do by forging the *edge* required to succeed.

That said, we must also acknowledge Kafka for his persistence – retaining and developing his self-expression even while locked in a repressive state. Most outsiders suppress and even extinguish their creativity for the sake of the *brotberuf*. And the fact Kafka didn't, despite everything, makes him more of a hero for me than the well-connected Orwell or the narcissistic Sartre.

Certainly, many outsiders are Kafkaesque with respect to their creativity. They view it as an inner frustration they'd fully explore if not for the *brotberuf*. Yet, as a utility for giving us the required *edge* to find and explore meaning, creativity is vital. No matter what form it takes, creativity is our best, perhaps only, escape from our mental prison. Yet to find the key it must be developed and honed to the point of profitability.

Creativity is something we cultivate – usually through what's termed the 'creative process'. Indeed, there's a definite path for encouraging unique thoughts and ideas, as well as their application. Yet many outsiders struggle with creativity, often because they don't know where to begin. One way around this is to 'begin with the end in mind' (in fact, one of Stephen Covey's famous habits in *The Seven Habits of Highly Effective People* (1989)). This simply means calculating – or perhaps visualizing (i.e imagining the final form) – what we're trying to achieve, and for what purpose. And only then considering what's involved in its execution.

Perhaps it's an artistic pursuit – a song, sculpture or short film, say – or something more functional, such as a new product or design for an existing product. Or it could be a new way of expressing a concept (a common requirement in my public relations company). Whatever: some visualization of the end product is a necessary start, even if the finished article's ultimately a long way from our original vision.

Being open to uncertainty

Visualizing the end-result is as prescriptive as we should get for the moment, however, because the creative process is all about opening ourselves up to uncertainty.

'Whatever we can do to expand our capacity for uncertainty is wonderful preparation for creativity,' says Julie Burstein, author of *Spark: How Creativity Works* (2011). 'One key element is what poet

John Keats called "negative capability". Here you don't know what's going to happen next but are nonetheless willing to chase down ideas and also willing to understand that not all of them will lead somewhere. But the experience of pursuing an idea will influence the next idea.'

Of course, this can sound woolly, something Burstein's well-aware of, which leads to the next stage in the creative process:

'At a certain point you have to sit down and do the work,' she explains.

By this, Burstein means we have to write it down, or sketch it or in some other way generate a first draft. And that takes us to the next important stage, though one often missed by outsiders: sharing.

'Understanding how you can share your work is a key part of the creative process,' confirms Burstein.

Indeed, it's *the* requirement for these early endeavours if we're not to spend our life blunted in Kafkaesque frustration. Yet sharing can lead to rejection – perhaps the airing of the 'fatal flaw' we'd failed to notice. Certainly, outsiders are often sensitive souls that dislike criticism, meaning we're vulnerable to collapse at the first negative comment. In fact, for many outsiders the term 'constructive criticism' is a contradiction in terms.

Nonetheless, if our creativity's to become profitable it *must* see the light of day.

The art of thought

Recognizing each element of the process – as well as generating a structure that formalizes these creative steps – is, therefore, important if we're not to fall at the first setback or criticism. In fact, such a process puts negativity – perhaps emerging from Burstein's 'sharing' – in its rightful place as just one part of a dynamic mechanism for developing ideas.

Yet Burstein's steps follow a tradition for formalizing creativity going back decades. Most famously, London School of Economics psychologist Graham Wallas (1858–1932) published *The Art of Thought* in 1926 – outlining the five stages of the creative process. These are:

Preparation. During this stage the problem is 'investigated in all directions'. The aim is to prepare the thinker by accumulating all the intellectual resources required. It's a corralling of 'stuff' – a gathering of what may be useful, though not in any order or structure. This can be on a big table with what's relevant heaped high and scattered wide, although it can also be a file or folder (though printed rather than electronic). Also for preparation, we need to define our goal: what's the deliverable – the problem to be solved or the consumable to be manufactured?

Incubation. Now we need to process the 'stuff', although – curiously – a key need here is to *not* directly focus on the problem at hand. There are two divergent elements to this stage, notes Wallas: the 'negative fact', which is our conscious avoidance of thinking about a particular problem; and the 'positive fact' of unconscious or involuntary gestation. Somewhere in our head we're still tangentially seeking an answer.

Yes, Wallas is telling us to go and do something else. And if this seems frustrating or inefficient we can perhaps use the time to kick-start another creative project – meaning we've several collation-and-gestation processes ongoing simultaneously. At no point, however, should we seek to complete a single idea or creative project in one session. Instead, we should allow a particularly lucid period to run on while recognizing this will eventually stall, which is no more than a positive signal to switch projects.

Intimation. The incubation has done its job. We're now agitating to focus on a particular project, not least because we suspect we're on the brink of . . .

Illumination. This is our eureka-moment, according to Wallas. The interruptions and distractions have generated the required insights – most likely to emerge from the subliminal self, especially if we've prepared well. That said, illumination is not always a flash of insight – otherwise, we'd wait impatiently and fruitlessly for something to pop into our head. Instead, Wallas describes it as the 'culmination of a successful train of association, which may have lasted for an appreciable time'.

In other words, one thought leads to another – exactly as Burstein describes. The point is to capture the thoughts and keep going, hoping there are as many leaps as there are dead ends.

Verification. And finally there's the validation of the idea. This involves reducing it to a form we can examine as a potential prototype or draft. Inevitably, this will include Burstein's sharing.

Of course, we could stay in the dark at the *illumination* stage, which may be a result of poor *preparation*, or maybe we were too uptight, restricting lucid thoughts at the *incubation* stage. In fact, we should recognize that all the stages need time to work and interplay with each other, meaning that it's our awareness of their distinct roles that matters more than any strict demarcation in terms of order.

A technique for producing ideas

Unfortunately, *The Art of Thought* is out of print, although another famous work on the subject is available: James Webb Young's *A Technique for Producing Ideas* (1965). Written for the burgeoning 1960s advertising industry, Webb Young claims that 'the production of ideas is as definite a process as the production of Fords'.

In fact, his step-by-step methodology should, by now, feel rather familiar.

* First, gather all the raw materials relating to our immediate problem.
* Second, tear them apart in ways that allow for easy and quick reference. He suggests writing notes on those 6×4-inch indexing cards or in a scrap book.
* Next, mull over the information, noticing different, not necessarily relevant, aspects.

- Then incubate, again through distraction. Webb Young cites Sherlock Holmes dragging the irritated Watson to a concert during a tricky case.
- Finally, come back to the information afresh before finding the key insight and developing it into its final shape.

Yet there's also room for some chaos when it comes to creativity – even silliness. In his famous book *It's Not How Good You Are, It's How Good You Want To Be* (2003) advertising creative Paul Arden (1940–2008) offers the following ideas for getting the juices flowing:

- Do the opposite to what you think the solution requires.
- Change your tools: paint rather than sketch, scribble rather than type.
- Look out the window and make whatever catches your eye – a bird, a television aerial, an old man on crutches – the solution to your problem.

Drowning creativity: our education system

Creativity can therefore be both formulaic and anarchic. So it's interesting that creativity can feel so alien to so many people – especially outsiders forced to suppress their creativity for the *brotberuf*. Yet it's hardly surprising we struggle to be creative given the way most westerners are educated. At least, that's the contention of renowned educational-evangelist Sir Ken Robinson.

In a series of books and lectures, Robinson has become a thorn in the side of educational establishments on both sides of the Atlantic. He contends that our education is modelled in the interests of industrialization, and in the image of it, which in our post-industrial landscape is both destroying our creativity, and all but useless.

'We have a production-line mentality to learning,' says Robinson. 'We operate education systems on the guiding principle of conformity – producing batches of children in certain age groups essentially conforming to certain standards.'

This makes education linear – starting a child at A with the aim of getting them to Z, which means testing and judging them on their speed of progress along this well-worn path. It also assumes there's a correct answer to every question, says Robinson, and that the aim of education is to ensure each child can absorb and recall the answer by a process of deductive reasoning.

According to Robinson, such methodology virtually extinguishes creativity. As proof he cites experiments in 'divergent thinking' on 5, 10 and 15-year-olds by creative researchers George Land and Beth Jarman. Divergent thinking is a child's capacity for creativity and originality. And while in Land and Jarman's tests an impressive 98 per cent of five-year-olds scored at 'genius' level, by the age of 10 the 'genius' quota had dropped to 32 per cent, which fell to just 10 per cent by 15.

'So they start with the capacity for creativity and it mostly deteriorates,' says Robinson. 'Why? Because they've become educated. They've been told there's only one answer.'

A hopeful message for outsiders

Far from an anti-establishment rant, Robinson's views on creativity offer a fantastically hopeful message for outsiders in my opinion – many of whom will have traced their alienation back to the classroom. It says the narrow bandwidth of our education system was the issue, *not* our inner turmoil or wayward thinking.

'Human intelligence is wonderfully diverse and multifarious,' says Robinson. 'We think about the world in all the ways we experience it. We think visually, in sound, kinaesthetically [through feeling]; we think in abstract and in terms of movement. Human intelligence is also dynamic and wonderfully interactive, with original thinking often coming from the interaction between different ways of seeing things [just as Burstein *et al.* described]. This makes the principle of diversity crucial for human development – something that is countered by our educational systems.'

According to Robinson, such systems are responsible for so many people leaving education assuming they're stupid. Yet they're far from stupid. Their brains simply work in ways not suited to the linear, logical, propositional and conformist educational structure we inject into every child subjected to the production line.

'Everywhere I go I find the same paradox,' Robinson writes in *Out of Our Minds* (2011). 'Most children think they're highly creative; most adults think they're not.'

Creativity has been beaten out of them, an appalling consequence of an education system that thwarted outsiders have every right to resent. Little wonder so many creative people think they're outsiders. Little wonder, also, that so many outsiders suppress their creativity for the sake of the *brotberuf*, rather than pursue their creativity in order to develop meaningful careers in something they love (helping them forge an *edge* in the process).

Make your creativity profitable

In fact, our creativity can become so suppressed it becomes our hidden passion, as it did for me. As a child I spent many hours alone in my bedroom inventing a made-up country. This started as a means of playing the football game *Subbuteo* on my own – something I found preferable to playing it socially. Yet results such as 'Liverpool 0, West Ham 10' were starting to look unrealistic, meaning I needed alternative teams. And this – ultimately – required a surrogate geography, which over the years led to an invented politics and an entirely made-up history.

Economic and industrial structures followed – as did culture, the media, even celebrities. I became interested in constitutional arrangements, public-sector budgets, financial markets, town-planning, architecture, international treaties, rural heritage, social divisions, and even artistic movements – all based on how I could apply each discipline to my entirely-concocted alternative world.

It was wonderfully creative. Yet it was also my guilty secret, especially as I became more and more lost in its intricacies and less and less interested in the thin academic fare on offer at my low-grade comprehensive school.

My father (a structural engineer) took a dim view. Although he confessed doing something similar when he was a child, his creativity was sacrificed for the sake of career conformity. And he expected me to do the same – even writing 'you are sacrificing your career' on the cover of the book in which I updated the football results and newspaper headlines. He was right, of course – I *was* sacrificing my career. Yet this was partly because my formal 'education' was incapable of accommodating such all-encompassing creativity, and partly because of my own failure to find a public, shareable, outlet for my original thinking.

Several years prior and just a few streets away, Turner Prize-winning artist and cross-dressing outsider Grayson Perry was lost within his own alternative universe (clearly a common response to the cultural desolation of exurban Essex). His world was dominated by his worn-out teddy bear: Emperor Alan Measles.

'I lived in Alan Measles's realm, carrying it around with me like a comfy sleeping bag I could pop into at any time,' he writes in his autobiography (written with Wendy Jones), *The Portrait of the Artist as a Young Girl* (2007). 'I held my make-believe world in my head, returning into it to find ready-formed landscapes, narratives and relationships. . . . I no longer had separate games they were all facets of the one game: everything was linked to this domain where Alan Measles was a major player.'

Perry went on to use his alternative world in his ground-breaking creativity as an acclaimed and highly-original ceramics artist. And who knows – if my father had, instead, written on my book 'make this creativity profitable' the results could have also been highly-original and transformative.

9
LEARNING TO PITCH

Hmm, sharing. It's a tough one for outsiders. It's asking outsiders to be judged by insiders – something certain to raise our defences. Yet forging an *edge* as a disadvantaged outsider requires some compromises, probably the most important of which is the need for others to invest in our output.

Painful as it is, the only way to make our creativity profitable is to present our work to those that hold the keys to our future. Whether it's funding, resources, knowledge, distribution, publicity – or something as mundane as a job – behind *their* door lies what *we* need. And it's usually via the 'pitch' that we'll get across the threshold.

However termed, a pitch – which can include a job interview – is a sales meeting involving others buying our ideas, products or labour. This is Burstein's 'sharing' *times 100* because it's not their feedback we seek – perhaps while honing the idea or concept – it's their investment.

Oh yes, this is a scary moment alright. Best do some prep.

Life's a pitch

At least that's the advice of design guru Stephen Bayley and advertising executive Roger Mavity. In their famous 2007 book *Life's a Pitch*, Bayley and Mavity do not exaggerate the central importance of the pitch to our progress in life: it's MASSIVE.

'Life is not a pattern of gradually evolving improvement,' they write. 'It's a series of long fallow patches punctuated by moments of crucial change. How you handle the long fallow stretches doesn't matter much. How you handle the moments of change is vital.'

Given that those moments are usually via pitching our work, Bayley and Mavity insist we understand the purpose of the pitch, as well as its structure and psychology. Depressingly, they also ask us to realize that any pitch is about judgement and decisions. It's us being judged, as much as our product or output, and the decisions others make can change our life.

'If you get the pitch right, everything follows,' they conclude. 'And if you don't, nothing follows.'

This is a painful realization for outsiders because we have to face the very thing we fear most: the judgement of others. Yet we must remember that such moments are not decided by luck or chance. They're decided by how we handle them. Win or lose, they're our responsibility, which – of course – seems unfair given that outsiders can feel uncomfortable in their own skin and probably never wanted to project themselves forward in the first place. But it also puts the outcome in our hands, allowing us to make our own progress towards finding meaning – as well as forging that *edge* – rather than relying on others.

The principles of pitching

Bayley and Mavity are not alone in writing iconic texts about pitching. Paul Arden's classic *It's Not How Good You Are, It's How Good You Want To Be* also covers pitching, as does *To Sell is Human* (2012) by workplace philosopher Daniel Pink. And, more recently, there's *Pitch Perfect* (2014) by US TV news anchor Bill McGowan, as well as *How to Win* (2014) by UK lifecoach Dr Rob Yeung. Their thoughts, and mine (from many years of pitching) are boiled down to 10 easily-digested principles below.

Principle one: It's theatre

'A pitch does not take place in the library of the mind but in the theatre of the heart,' write Bayley and Mavity.

Of course, many outsiders are introverts, so describing pitching as theatre can trigger fears that send us right back to our bedrooms. Yet all's not what it seems. They're not asking us to ham-up our pitch with Shakespearean language or exaggerated body and facial movements. Their plea is that we make presentations visual.

Don't tell them your idea, show them – a notion Paul Arden agrees with:

'Instead of giving people the benefit of your wit and wisdom (words) try painting them a picture,' he writes in *It's Not How Good You Are*. . . . 'The more strikingly visual your presentation is, the more people will remember it.'

Bill McGowan calls this his 'Scorsese Principle', after the famous movie director. Martin Scorsese uses imagery to illustrate a point – one example being the iconic jail scene in his cult-classic *Goodfellas* (1990). The camera focuses on mafia boss Paulie thinly-slicing garlic using a razor-blade – perfectly depicting the 'wise guys' living like kings while incarcerated.

'You are the director of your own product or company story,' says McGowan. 'What are the images that will bring your message to life?'

Principle two: Content is key

'Think playwright, not actor,' write Bayley and Mavity – again supporting the notion that we don't need to turn our pitch into a cringeworthy 'am-dram' performance to get our message across. But we do need to make sure the content is well argued, well delivered and compelling. Content matters, they state. In fact, poor content will be punished far more than poor delivery.

'Delivering a presentation well (the acting bit) is a useful skill, and one that can be learnt surprisingly easily,' say Bayley and Mavity, 'but what really matters is the playwright's skill; the ability to write a great presentation in the first place.'

This means deciding the key points to get across and how they can be framed in the most compelling way possible. Convoluted statements about technicalities will fail to ignite their interest. Meanwhile, compelling phrases that generate strong visual imagery can fire-up even the most jaded of audiences – no matter how flat the delivery (though some animation no doubt helps).

In fact, we should tell a story. At least that's the suggestion of Dr Rob Yeung. Stories are both memorable and persuasive, he says. They've an irrational appeal – bypassing defences by bringing in emotions and imagery that graphs and statistics cannot generate.

So how do we tell our story? Here Yeung employs the helpful mnemonic SOAR:

- *Situation:* what's the background to the story?
- *Obstacles:* what are the barriers the protagonists have to contend with – what researchers call the 'Underdog Effect', meaning that every good story involves a struggle?
- *Actions:* how do they deal with the barriers?
- *Resolution:* what's the result and what's been learnt?

Struggling to think of a story to tell? Here are some typical ones we use – depending on the audience – when pitching for public relations contracts.

- How and why Moorgate (our PR firm) was created.
- What lies behind Moorgate's values.
- How we generated the pitch we're about to present.
- How we came to understand your problem.
- How we helped a similar client.

Of course, the last of these is a case study, one of the most common stories in any sales process – not least because a case study tells the listener (a) they're not alone, (b) you understand their need, (c) there's a solution, and (d) you've solved it before.

That's a pretty strong story.

Principle three: Spend time thinking

'Above all, there needs to be time spent on *thinking*,' write Bayley and Mavity. 'This may seem utterly obvious, but in practice it's often neglected.'

My agreement with this principle comes, I'm afraid, from bitter experience. If I allow myself too short a timeframe for thinking about both the content and structure of a pitch it invariably falls flat. Some time and focus, however, are sure to be rewarded with useable ideas as well as a strong structure for presenting them. We must be ruthless with our diaries, state Bayley and Mavity, throwing out all the unwanted engagements in order to give ourselves time to think. As with the creative process, this includes enough time to go down blind alleys.

Of course, by 'thinking', the pitch gurus are really asking us to prepare well. Again, this may seem obvious, although it's surprising the number of people that fail to prepare at all, assuming they'll 'wing it' or recycle a previous pitch.

So what's the correct prep? For a start, we should study our audience . . .

Principle four: Focus on the audience

There's little to be gained from waltzing in and giving them a blast of positivity about your products, skill or art when it's irrelevant to their needs. So focus the pitch – not on you – but on *them*. Who are they, what's their problem, and how can you solve it?

This takes some research. But most of all it requires a change in perspective – what Daniel Pink calls 'attunement'.

'Attunement is the ability to bring one's actions and outlook into harmony with other people and with the context you're in,' says Pink.

When confronted with something new, are we attuned to the perspective of others, or simply ourselves? Pink cites experiments by social psychologists – one being the famous 'E-test' in which people are asked to draw an E on their forehead. Those drawing an outward-facing E – that can be read by others – are judged as more attuned to others' perspective than those drawing the E so that it's correct from their own viewpoint.

Attunement is clearly important. Yet it's often something outsiders lack. So how do we get it? According to Pink, it depends on three principles.

First, we should have *less power*. Yes, that's right: E-tests examining the relationship between perspective and power found that those with more power – perhaps in an office hierarchy – were more likely to draw the self-oriented E. Having less power is therefore good for our attunement with others' needs.

Round one to the outsider.

Second, we should *use our head as much as our heart*, says Pink. He cites mock business school negotiations in which one group is asked to negotiate after imagining what the other side is *feeling*, while another must pursue talks based on what it reasons the other side is *thinking*. Meanwhile, a third 'control' group is instructed to not consider the other side at all.

Of course, both groups easily beat the control group of inconsiderate negotiators. Yet those assessing thoughts consistently beat those focusing on feelings, making rationality at least as important as empathy – again, a conclusion likely to suit us empathy-distorting outsiders.

Third, we must *mimic strategically*. Humans mimic each other – perhaps in speech or body language – naturally as part of our social glue, say anthropologists: a trait going back to early man looking for trustworthy signals from those they encountered. Yet in modern times mimicry is often used in sales environments, with staff in the retail and hospitality industries sometimes trained in the art.

'We're more likely to be persuaded by those whom we like,' writes Pink. 'And one reason we like people is that they remind us of . . . us.'

Yet mimicry requires a deft touch if it's not to come across as a clumsy ploy.

Principle five: Follow a structure
We must structure what we want to say. This sounds obvious, yet it's often neglected – resulting in pitches that fail to build a story or

answer a need or ignite the interest of those on the receiving end of our unstructured and therefore rambling pitch. As Bayley and Mavity write, 'a housebuilder starts with a blueprint, not a catalogue of roof-tile designs'.

So we must follow a clear structure for communicating our ideas.

Bayley and Mavity cite the British Army's doctrine on how to communicate: 'Say what you're going to say. Say it. Say it again'. Or we can follow Rob Yeung's SOAR mnemonic – situation, obstacles, actions, resolution – which at least acknowledges the narrative needs of a pitch. Certainly, at Moorgate we follow something similar – with our pitches structured to have:

1. A *premise*, in which we state why we're there and what we're about to present.
2. *Objectives*, in which we set out our goals. As a PR agency, these usually involve raising the profile of our clients, although it's here where their needs can be outlined, as well as any barriers or problems we're aiming to solve.
3. *Audiences.* Who are we trying to influence?
4. *Messages.* Here come the sales points and benefits.
5. A *strategy.* What's our overall plan for execution?
6. Some *tactics* or action points. These should cover, perhaps, the first six months.

Principle six: Make simplicity an obsession

'You've got to concentrate on the few things that really matter,' write Bayley and Mavity. 'That is why [winners] keep it simple . . . The simpler your idea and the simpler your presentation of it, then the more likely you are to emerge the winner.'

McGowan calls this the 'Pasta Sauce Principle' – the notion that every sauce is better when it's boiled down to its essence.

'You should make your message as rich and brief as you possibly can,' he states. 'Avoid the temptation to overwhelm your audience. Leave them hungry for more.'

In fact, we should leave them with a single message – what in entrepreneurial circles is known as the 'elevator pitch' (i.e. what we'd say to a key investor if given just seconds to say it).

According to Pink, this can be distilled even further, perhaps down to the . . .

. . . *one-two word pitch* – or perhaps a strapline. Our PR firm uses 'communicating expertise', which summarizes our offering better than any other two words we can think of . . .

. . . *question pitch* that leaves your audience assuming you're the answer. Pink cites Ronald Reagan's 1980 election slogan: 'Are you better off now than you were four years ago?' . . .

. . . *subject line pitch*. Think about the subject lines of emails, now the near-universal tool for winning pitch meetings. Distillation's essential, and helpful . . .

. . . *the Twitter pitch*. This is the same as the subject-line pitch, although reduces the message to 140 characters. 'The best pitches are short, sweet and easy to retweet,' rhymes Pink, bringing us to the . . . .

. . . *rhyming pitch*. Certainly, these are memorable – boosting cognitive 'processing fluency'. To this day I can remember the words of the 1970s advertisement for *Matey* bubble bath ('Your Matey's a bottle of fun; you slips me in the bath; I'm loved by everyone; I'm always good for a laugh . . . ') – even teaching it to my kids 30 years later. That's one powerful pitch!

Principle seven: Perfection's not what they're after
Defining the problem is often more important than presenting an exact solution: not least because – as they know and you'll discover – everything changes in execution. This is something you must also accept of your product or talent. But it's not something to be greeted negatively. As Paul Arden states:

> 'If you show a client a highly polished computer layout, he will probably reject it. There is either too much to worry about or not enough to worry about. They are equally bad. It is a *fait accompli*. There is nothing for him to do. It's not his work. He doesn't feel involved.'

In fact, this is a key moment in any pitch – when they start adding *their* input to your idea, or even your skills. Of course, outsiders can react defensively, perhaps seeing it as an interruption or assuming it's a criticism or even that they're being attacked. Usually, it's the opposite: it's them aligning themselves with your potential – something requiring a *growth mindset* to spot.

Go with the flow – appreciate the wisdom on offer (whatever you feel inside) – and watch that threshold loom into view.

Principle eight: Delivery and body language matters

'If they don't have confidence in you, they certainly won't have confidence in your idea,' write Bayley and Mavity.

Of course, this feels immediately disabling for outsiders who, no matter what the veneer, can feel deeply under-confident within (hence the defensiveness). Yet outward confidence is something we can construct by following a few simple rules:

- *Don't try too hard.* 'People who look as if they are desperate to reassure you only end up looking desperate,' say Bayley and Mavity, who state that part of the challenge is to look as if it doesn't matter. Don't look lazy or unbothered, but avoid looking as if your life depends on it.
- *Go in as an equal.* Being overly toady will more likely inspire contempt than confidence. 'Your tone and body language must suggest that we are all looking at this problem as equals together,' say Bayley and Mavity. That said, some acknowledgement of their skills and experience will go a long way.
- *Understand a few simple things*, and present them. Don't overload the pitch with statistics and analysis that you may have trouble explaining. That way you'll know the material, and lose that nagging 'imposter' fear of being found out.
- *Focus on dependability.* They're buying you, not the product (see below), and they want to know you can deliver: so make that your focus – perhaps via a case study that demonstrates previous reliability.

- *Slow down.* This is one of my worst failings – galloping through a presentation so I come across as a fretful mouse rather than a commanding lion. To counter, I inject some deliberate pausing or ask 'any questions?' every few minutes (encouraging their input).
- *Posture.* Yes – all the usual tips on body language. Walk boldly, stand tall, sit up straight, shake hands firmly, look interested, develop strong eye contact (at everyone, not just the boss), don't splay your legs (if a man) or fold your arms or play with your cuffs/necklace/pen.
- *Dress well.* The clothing *faux pas* is probably the quickest way to lose confidence in a pitch meeting, though many of the judgements are revealed via side comments or humour. I've seen it all: men wearing 'distressed' jeans or a waiter's suit, women wearing clothes meant for a hen night. If in doubt, research what you think they'll be wearing – and get as close to that as you can (classic tribal signalling, in other words).

Principle nine: Remember they're buying you, not the solution/product

Bayley and Mavity make the point that they're buying you as much as your solution.

'Again and again, when people are asked to back a plan, in reality they are being asked to back the person behind the plan,' they write. 'That's why trust and confidence [in you] are so important.'

A recurring observation in *Life's a Pitch* is that the final advertising campaign is rarely the one used in the pitch by the winning team. In other words – and despite appearances – what's being chosen is not the product being sold but the team presenting it (that's you).

So what are they looking for? The gurus all seem to agree on this: they're looking for someone they can work with.

Principle ten: Welcome the questions

Some of the most difficult pitches I've experienced involved being interrogated. Add a lamp and cigarette smoke and the scene could be straight from a TV cop show. Disbelief, sarcasm, insults: I've had the lot. Meanwhile, some of the easiest pitches I've made involved no questions at all. I've run smoothly through my presentation, been smiled at, thanked, and left feeling great.

And a week later I've receive a rejection email. Meanwhile, those interrogations usually end in a deal.

Questions – including seemingly nasty ones – are what sales people call 'buying signals'. Even negative feedback has the upside that they're taking it seriously, no matter how it looks at the time.

'A pitch is a good pitch when people start taking an active part in the process,' say Bayley and Mavity. 'So questions matter greatly. They are not an intrusion, they are an involvement.'

Certainly, we should answer questions straightaway rather than insist on completing our presentation. In fact, screw the presentation: once they're talking it's done its job. And if they've pre-empted your next point – say so. Compliment them for being 'ahead of the game' – they'll glow in the acclaim and start seeing you as someone they can work with.

As for the negativity – well, just occasionally it's as bad as it sounds. Yet even here we should be grateful: allowing us to write-off this 'car-crash' by turning it into a learning exercise for the next pitch. And, yes, there will be a next pitch. There's always someone else. The only way there won't be is if you – too bruised – skulk back to your mental cave and stay there.

Finally, be aware that no one will give you a definitive 'yes' at the first meeting, so your task at this stage is to not elicit a definite 'no'. Only after the third meeting – with no definite 'yes' – should you become concerned about the length of time the process is taking. Obviously, after a certain point further meetings are more likely to go against you than in your favour – with the exception of many recruitment processes. HR departments, these days, are notorious for adding layer upon layer – meeting on top of assessment on top of dinner or awayday. My enrolment as a banker, for instance, involved seven interviews, two dinners, a lunch, a 'drinking session' and an all-day 'offsite': a tough call for an outsider spending the entire time battling imposter phenomenon.

10 Principles for Pitching

1. *Make it theatre – and make it visual.*
2. *Content is key – tell a strong story.*
3. *Spend time thinking – preparation matters.*
4. *Focus on the audience – attune to their needs.*
5. *Follow a structure – it's crucial to being understood.*
6. *Make simplicity an obsession – i.e. cut the crap.*
7. *Perfection's not what they're after – they want some input.*
8. *Delivery and body language matters – as ever.*
9. *Remember they're buying you, not the solution/product.*
10. *Welcome the questions – they're buying signals.*

10

GETTING STRATEGIC

In 1997 I ended an eight-year relationship with a woman I'd met at university. The break-up was my fault. I'd become a banker, so finally had some money in my pocket. I'd also filled-out physically and developed a degree of aptitude when communicating with the opposite sex (from a very low base). Basically – having gained a degree of confidence – I was keen to explore its potential: a common cause of male-instigated relationship breakdown for similarly-aged couples in their 30s.

On noticing my restlessness, my employers – mostly men in their 40s (many having been through the same process) – decided I was the perfect man to fill their vacancy in New York: world epicentre of restless outsiders. Of course, I'd loved the city since my first reading of *The Catcher in the Rye*, so jumped at the chance.

I'd been a regular visitor while a journalist. Staying in the company apartment bang next to the World Trade Center, I'd wandered the mean streets: hands in pockets, collar up and with the weight of the world on my shoulders. And, while perhaps a little old for mimicking Caulfield, I felt every bit the James Dean poster-boy of Times Square, even if I had to keep one eye on the time for the next scheduled meeting.

Yet the bank had moved to suburban Greenwich, Connecticut. This meant a 40-minute 'reverse commute' and some restrictions over my choice of 'hood' – settling on the Upper West Side because it was within easy reach of 125th Street station and due to the area's iconic brownstone mansion blocks. And commuting in those uncrowded litter-strewn trains allowed me time to reflect on my experiences living in the outsider's very own holy city. Inevitably (for a former journo) my thoughts turned into scribbled notes, which were typed up in the evenings. Soon enough, I had around 40,000 words, a synopsis for a book, and was looking for a literary agent.

Technology was now on my side, with the inevitable email rejection letters offering the chance for a conversation. So I asked one for advice on finding the right agent.

'Find the closest writer to your style, and lobby their agent,' he said.

It was good advice. As well as New York, the book focused on my rapidly-collapsing banking career, which had been hit by the 1998 emerging market debt crisis, as well as my dalliances within New York's idiosyncratic dating scene. It was humorous and self-deprecating. But it was most definitely male. So I targeted Nick Hornby's agent. She bit, and in short-order we landed a deal with one of the Britain's largest and most respected publishers.

I'd combined my outsider creativity with my journalistic training – giving me the *edge* required to become a 'lad-lit' author. I was in Heaven. Less than a year later, however, and it was Hell I entered. To my amazement, the book was condemned as 'sexist' – not helped by the front cover image of a man in Union Jack boxershorts. What's more, its distasteful tone meant it was ignored by book reviewers, and was even mocked by friends for its excruciating sexual detail.

The publisher – who I'd befriended in the run-up to publication – stopped returning my calls and ignored my emails. And even my agent, who'd shown remarkable patience during my overly-emotional post-publication collapse, went quiet, bringing an end to my creative dream.

My *edge* blunted, I slunk back into my outsider cave.

The false breakthrough

The above story is a classic example of a 'false breakthrough': one of the most demoralizing yet common disasters to befall outsiders seeking meaning through creativity.

We develop goals. We plan. We throw everything at pitching until we win that breakthrough opportunity. *Fantastic* – we think – we're on our way, only for it to fall from our grasp during execution. Despite our best efforts at delivery, and our increasingly desperate attempts to save the situation, the opportunity's lost – sending us back to square one though now with a major defeat to contemplate.

And while there's no way of guaranteeing we can avoid such a fate, the best way of reducing its potential is to adopt a strong strategy for execution. Looking back, I certainly had no strategy. I had a book, which was no more than a reasonable start on my long journey towards what should have been my goal of becoming an author.

Of course, I had a strategy for winning a book deal: I'd produce most of what's required and then find the right agent. But what then? I was way too dependent on my one product as a breakthrough, when it was me – the writer – they were judging. A judgement wrecked, what's more, by my increasingly-desperate attempts to save what I'd convinced myself was my once-in-a-lifetime chance at fulfilling my creative dream.

What is a strategy?

Only now can I see the mistake. Only now do I realize that the right strategy is vital for both winning opportunities and consolidating them through strong execution. Indeed, despite appearances, the initial breakthrough is the easy bit. People are often on the lookout for the new-new thing. And they'll admire your bravery and guile for getting through the door as much as they'll like your creativity.

Delivery, meanwhile – especially over the long term – is a lot harder, hence the need for a thought-through long-term strategy.

This leaves us trying to find the right strategy, although it also leaves us potentially asking what, exactly, is a strategy? This is an odd question because the dictionary definition is quite clear. It's 'a plan, method, or series of manoeuvres or stratagems for obtaining a specific goal'. So, having developed our goals, the strategy is our plan of action for achieving them – ensuring that each action is, indeed, focused on our objectives.

That's a perfectly adequate description in my opinion, although one missed by a large number of those espousing strategies. This is especially true in the corporate world where the word 'strategy' crops up on a near-daily basis. In fact, many companies make serious errors when settling on a strategy, often without even realizing it. At least that's the view of leading US corporate strategist Richard Rumelt. In his highly-accessible 2011 book *Good Strategy/Bad Strategy*, Rumelt rails against what he views as the majority of companies making crass errors when focusing on a strategy.

Statements such as 'our strategy is to be the best at making doughnuts in the Tristate area' or 'our strategy is to sell the most sunglasses in the Midwest' irritate Rumelt greatly, because they're not strategies at all. They're 'statements of desire', which for him means they're 'bad strategy'.

'Most businesspeople don't know how to strategize,' says Rumelt. 'They think it means listing goals. They're not even close.'

Yet listing goals isn't the only *bête noire* for Rumelt when it comes to strategy. Others include those that . . .

. . . *contain 'fluff'*, which he describes as a 'form of gibberish masquerading as strategic concepts or arguments'. This usually involves using words that are 'inflated and unnecessarily abstruse'. Some are obvious, such as 'the best', or 'leading', or 'excellent', but others such as 'unorthodox' or 'imaginative' hide the fact they're little more than hyperbole. Real strategies deal with the 'how' not just the 'want' – something requiring clarity and brevity when using language . . .

. . . fail to face the challenge. 'When you cannot define the challenge, you cannot evaluate a strategy to improve it,' says Rumelt. This leaves many strategies little better than the carthorse Boxer's maxim in George Orwell's *Animal Farm* (1945): 'I will work harder'. If directionless, such a strategy simply digs us deeper into the wrong hole: exactly my problem with the book. I saw its success as the solitary goal, when it was merely a stepping-stone to the real objective of becoming a writer . . .

. . . suggest impractical solutions. If your strategy cannot be implemented, it's – again – more a statement of desire than a strategic plan, opines Rumelt. And while this sounds obvious, it's also the common error of companies and people bullied into assuming 'thinking big' is the key guarantor of success.

Good strategy

Yet Rumelt's message is far from negative.

'Once you develop the ability to detect bad strategy,' he states, 'you will dramatically improve your effectiveness at judging, influencing and creating [good] strategy.'

'Good strategy is coherent action backed up by an argument,' says Rumelt, 'an effective mixture of thought and action with a basic underlying structure.'

To explain, he turns to one of his strategic heroes: Apple's Steve Jobs (1955–2011). In fact, this biological son of Syrian-Swiss students (forced to put him up for adoption); this adopted child of a mechanic and a payroll clerk; this school maverick and college dropout; and this part Buddhist-hippie vegan, part socially-awkward computer-geek, should also be one of our heroes – not least because he always considered himself an outsider.

Yet he was an outsider with an *edge*: a clear strategic vision, at least during his second spell as the boss of Apple Inc. As Rumelt explains, after the 1995 release of Microsoft's *Windows 95*, Apple 'fell into a death spiral'. And by September 1997 the company was just two months from bankruptcy, with analysts urging it to throw in the towel or sell up to a 'major' – Apple's market share having fallen to just 3 per cent.

It was at this point co-founder Steve Jobs returned as interim CEO. Most assumed it was to oversee the company's sale or wind up. Yet within a year Jobs had set Apple on the path to becoming, 10 years later, the world's largest company by market valuation: something he achieved by adopting a clear, executable – Rumelt even calls it 'obvious' – strategy.

First, 'he cut Apple back to a core that could survive,' wrote Rumelt.

He turned 15 desktop models into one. He cut the myriad choice in laptops, also down to one. He cut out all the printers and peripherals. And he culled the engineers and software developers, as well as reduced the distributors and retailers.

Yet that was the easy bit – what Rumelt calls 'business 101'. What about sales? What about growth? Here he did two things, though Rumelt mentions only one in his excellent recounting of Apple's turnaround. Asked by Rumelt (in the summer of 1998) 'what's your strategy?' Jobs answered: 'I am going to wait for the next big thing'.

Of course, Jobs had a strong view of the tech horizon – seeing that the storm caused by Napster's musical-downloading website presented an opportunity for a downloading gizmo (the *iPod*); as did the rapidly-converging worlds of the mobile phone and the Internet (the *iPhone*).

But that wasn't all. In 1997, having just taken back the reins of the company, Jobs made a remarkable speech to the *Apple Worldwide Developers Conference*: then a demoralized convention hoping for a miracle (and only slowly realizing one was in their midst).

This is what he said:

'You've got to start with the customer experience and work backwards to the technology,' he told them. 'You can't start with the technology and try to figure out where you're going to try to sell it. . . . And as we have tried to come up with a strategy and a vision for Apple, it's started with: what incredible benefits we can give to the customer . . . We're not starting with – let's sit down with the engineers and figure out what awesome technology we have – and then how we're going to market that.'

So Jobs' strategy was crystal clear: to cut back (to survive), to focus on the customer experience (not least through good design), and to prepare for the 'next big thing'.

And the rest, as they say, is history.

The war analogy

It's the simplicity of Jobs' strategy that makes it so admirable for Rumelt. And it's simplicity we'll need as individuals if our strategy is to be effective, something that can be aided by our ability to visualize our strategy. While sounding silly, the fact Apple's workers could imagine themselves in a newly-built fortress – capable of sustaining attack but also allowing them to search the landscape for an opportune moment to break out – no doubt helped. It meant they understood the strategy, and were motivated by such an understanding.

I'm reminded of the Anglo-Saxon king, Alfred the Great. Reduced to the marsh-island fortress of Athelney (where he burnt the cakes) with a trusted band of diehards, they guarded against another attack while spying on the Danish camps and building covert armies for the counter-attack. When it came, the offensive swept the Vikings from southern England and saved the English (and their language) from annihilation.

In fact – and despite modern sensibilities – military analogies are perhaps the best way to visualize strategy. Certainly, they help us untangle the lines dividing objectives, strategies and tactics: that age-old dynamic all strategists should be aware of though many confuse. In war, the objective is obvious – victory. Strategies, meanwhile, are how we employ our resources to achieve that goal.

With few resources, Alfred the Great waited and plotted while building alliances with sympathetic villagers – not dissimilar to the Western Allies' strategy in the Cold War (knowing a full-on attack against the Soviet Union could end in nuclear Armageddon). In World War Two, however, the Allies opted for a strategy of 'total war', knowing that the Axis powers were overstretched and that America's productive power, along with the USSR's resourcefulness, could outstrip their capacity to replenish their depleting armaments.

The Cold War/WW2 comparison (and even Alfred the Great) reveals another interesting need when deciding on a strategy: that the best, most obvious, strategy relies on an assessment of our relative strengths and weaknesses. A hot war against the Soviets would have been pointless and wasteful because their nuclear and conventional weapons matched those of NATO's. Yet they were economically weak compared to the West, meaning containment and the long game would surely pay dividends. Likewise, both the Japanese and German war machines were limited, meaning neither could sustain 'total war' over the medium term.

Developing the right strategy

So how do we decide on a strategy as individuals – perhaps with few or no resources to employ, let alone armies? Rumelt talks about the 'kernel of good strategy' – the seeds or building blocks that both companies and individuals can use to generate executable strategies.

First, there's the *diagnosis*. This 'defines or explains the nature of the challenge'. Too often we're uncertain what we face, making good strategy impossible. In both WW2 and the Cold War it was an accurate assessment of the enemy that drove strategy. And, while peaceful pursuits are inevitably more complex, if we can reduce the need to a phrase or even word – 'survival' for Apple in 1997, for instance – we're immediately encouraging clear thinking.

Next comes the *guiding policy*. 'This is an overall approach chosen to cope with or overcome the obstacles identified in the diagnosis,' says Rumelt. 'Total war' counts in this respect, as does the 'containment' approach of the Cold War. Again, brevity helps. So does the critical avoidance of 'statements of desire'.

And finally there's the set of *coherent actions* (or tactics), aimed at executing the guiding policy. 'These are steps that are coordinated with one another to work together in accomplishing the guiding policy,' says Rumelt.

Desperate self-defeating behaviour

Given this, it's perhaps easier to understand why my early book-writing pursuits failed. It was my objective – to 'get published' – that led to the calamity. That was a mere milestone – a tactic – towards the real goal of becoming an established author. And given that I had the wrong objective, all else followed – hence my desperate and self-defeating behaviour.

Rather than develop contacts and win people over I alienated key people by focusing on one, failing, book. A book, what's more, that had already done its job of opening doors into the world I wanted to enter. Doors that soon slammed shut – not because the book failed (it actually sold well) – but because I saw that one book as my only chance, and behaved like an idiot when it didn't meet my unrealistic expectations.

In fact, the mistakes go back further still. Too keen to please, I'd allowed the book to be taken in a more sexual direction – abandoning much of the banking content. While part of the story, for sure, the book was a balance between 'banking and bonking', though one disrupted by the publisher who edited out some fascinating elements, including content that became relevant to the Enron scandal (thus restricting its potential market).

Yet I ignored my agent's warnings regarding the editing – assuming that, now I was 'in' with the publisher, her advice held less sway. She had my long-term interests in mind, however, even if I didn't. And she knew that Union Jack boxer-shorts were passé even for a lad-lit author in the late 1990s.

Helping you 'think different'

Finally, it's worth noting that a good strategy isn't just about executing the expression of your creativity, it can be its engine. Get the strategy right and your creativity's fired up – running on all cylinders. Get it wrong, however, and an early warning could be the evaporation of your creativity: certainly my post-book experience, resulting in a 10-year writer's block.

Yet there's hope. Just as I eventually learnt from the experience, using it to aid my second incarnation as a book writer, there's always a second chance, as long as we learn the lessons. Jobs' 'second coming' at Apple proves this point wonderfully. It allowed him to slay some ghosts from his previous stint as CEO as well as correct more than a few mistakes, which he readily admitted (another strong sign of a good strategist).

It also allowed him to focus on what Apple really meant to its customers. Having slimmed down to a single desktop – what would become the iconic *iMac* – and knowing it was probably the last throw of the dice, he positioned Apple as a celebration of its creativity, as well as both the company's and its customers' outsider status.

The *Think Different* campaign – conceived by advertising guru and Apple-diehard Lee Clow – was based on Jobs' vision and strategy for relaunching Apple as the user-oriented computer for creative and design-conscious people. The campaign included images of those who'd swum against the tide and changed history: Gandhi, Lennon, Dylan, Picasso and Martin Luther King among them.

And it included this piece of advertising copy – partly written by Jobs himself:

'Here's to the crazy ones. The misfits. The rebels. The troublemakers. The round pegs in square holes. The ones who see things differently. They're not fond of rules. And they have no respect for the status quo. You can quote them, disagree with them, glorify or vilify them. About the only thing you can't do is ignore them. Because they change things.

They push the human race forward. And while some may see them as the crazy ones, we see genius. Because the people who are crazy enough to think they can change the world are the ones who do.'

Of course, the above isn't a strategy. It's a positioning statement, though one giving Apple one hell of an *edge*. It also tells us that Apple under Jobs believed in maverick creativity as a strategy. This was a bold approach that, nonetheless, returned the company to its outsider roots: a message it reasoned its audience would appreciate, as any viewing of the company's sales figures from 1998 onwards proves.

The Strategic *Edge*

- *Beware the 'false breakthrough' of seemingly strong opportunities lost through pursuing the wrong (or even no) strategy.*
- *Bad strategies are often just 'statements of desire' or those that fail to face the challenge or suggest impractical solutions.*
- *Good strategies involve coherent actions backed up by a coherent argument – focused on an obtainable goal.*
- *Simplicity is a key need – aided by the ability to visualize our strategies.*
- *The best strategies also rely on an assessment of our relative strengths and weaknesses – and of theirs.*
- *Good strategy fires up your creativity, while bad strategy can kill it stone dead.*
- *Yet we must remember that there's always a second chance.*

11

USING JUDGEMENT

Judgement matters. Listen to the news and accusations of poor judgement are thrown around like punches in a brawl. Business leaders, politicians, celebrities: all are condemned on a daily basis for lacking judgement – a seemingly fatal flaw for those in positions of authority. A fatal flaw, what's more, that could be another defining characteristic of outsiders. Poor judgement hangs like an albatross around our necks – terrorizing our current decision-making while traumatizing our view of the past.

One problem is that outsiders – especially disadvantaged outsiders with poor educational benchmarks or parental mentoring – can feel overly-pressured when making judgements. First, we assume they're all-or-nothing decisions. Make the wrong call, and certain disaster follows. Second, we distrust most external inputs into the process – assuming they're false or that we've somehow misinterpreted them. And third, our 'gut instinct' is usually so polluted with fear and anger – and even self-hatred – that it's useless as a guiding light for our judgements. Indeed, many outsiders spend much of their time fighting – not 'going with' – their gut instinct.

Such a corrupted process makes us suspicious and defensive. Ironically, this can make outsiders good decision-makers when genuinely threatened or attacked. When it comes to advancement, however – perhaps finding and seizing opportunities – our judgement's awry. Too focused on the downside, we can fail to spot the upside, or become too fearful to make the leap.

That said, such defensiveness is one of two typical outsider responses. The other is bravado. Here, we ignore *any* consideration of risk before charging headlong into the fray. This may sound courageous but, in reality, it's no better than a Travis Bickle-style 'virtual suicide'. It's a poorly-judged disregard for the consequences that, while immediately energizing, usually ends in disaster.

What's missing is rational advancement: the cool assessment of the risks and rewards leading to well-considered decisions moving us steadily towards our goals – the downsides quantified, the upsides grounded and practical.

The emotional handicap

So why is judgement such a problem for outsiders? Some key reasons include:

Our emotions. Related to our sensitivity (mentioned in Chapter 1), emotions are a classic concern for outsiders – one with a potentially-biological root. For whatever reason, emotional people are usually overloaded on the stress hormone noradrenaline/norepinephrine. This agitates the amygdala – the brain's emotional regulator (found in the limbic system) – producing overly-emotional, usually fearful responses when triggered. Debate rages whether this is genetic or the result of early-life conditioning (perhaps trauma). Yet the result's the same: judgements dictated by emotional rather than rational considerations.

Either that or we suppress it – developing that other characteristic response of detachment, in which we become disinterested, perhaps by becoming 'super-cool' or even the geek or swot. Either way, our emotions are wrecking our judgement, which – in turn – blunts any potential *edge*.

Distrust. Fear leads to distrust. Again, poor early-life conditioning can prevent outsiders from discerning between those we can and cannot trust. This can make us too trusting – even naïve – when dealing with others. More usually, it prevents us accepting others' actions at face value – assuming they're concealing unstated motives that go against our interests, as well as feeding all those conspiracy theories we readily digest.

Of course, we invest time and energy searching for such motives and feel vindicated when we, inevitably, find them. Indeed, distrust can be a self-fulfilling prophecy (see below) – generating the very behaviours we suspect others are plotting, and therefore deepening our conviction that no-one can be trusted.

Low self-esteem. Both fear and distrust can be the result of low self-esteem: the root response to poor early-life conditioning. Assuming our abilities (or lack of them) innate – as with Dweck's *fixed mindset* – we develop poor self-beliefs that lead, ultimately, to self-hatred. Of course, if we don't like ourselves we expect others to feel the same, which – again – puts us immediately on the defensive. In fact, so fearful can we become of the negative judgement of others we can react both defensively *and* offensively. We assume the worst and plan for it while developing hair-trigger reactivity against perceived attacks – a highly-disabling attribute when it comes to decision-making.

Fear of failure. This is often the behavioural result of low self-esteem. If our poor self-beliefs generate the fear that we'll fail, we'll not pick up the phone or write that letter or email. As for pitch meetings – well, they're to be avoided at all costs. Certainly, we'll prepare concerned more about the 'killer question' – the one that floors us – than about aligning our goals with theirs. Indeed, those with fear of failure will judge a pitch a success if they somehow scrape through without being 'outed' as an imposter.

Fear of failure distorts our evaluation of situations, which can lead to self-sabotage. For instance, we may confess weaknesses in the hope others 'go easy' – something I can remember doing at crucial job interviews. Or we may pretend we don't care, or state we're 'happier among the troops than the officers' – all of which makes fear of failure a self-fulfilling and disabling trait and one disastrous for good judgement.

Prejudice. All the above can lead to perhaps the most destructive trait for good judgement: prejudice. By prejudice, I mean prejudging situations and people, and therefore making judgements that confirm our prejudices. For instance, if we assume someone cannot be trusted, we'll soon 'find' the evidence to prove it. This makes us closed rather than open-minded as well as reactive rather than proactive – both disastrous traits for good judgement. Make no mistake, if we evaluate a situation based on pre-judging it – any pre-judgement, including the assumption of prejudice against us – we'll find little more than the confirmation we're looking for.

Sure, in the warped world of the outsider this can be comforting. It can even provide a rare (if inverted) camaraderie with others: 'I failed because they don't like women/Muslims/northerners', etc. But it leaves outsiders imprisoned within their perceived prejudices – making us bitter and angry, as well as trapped within ever-decreasing circles.

Making better judgements

There are books in abundance on both judgement and decision-making – many taking us through the logical processes involved: contextual-analysis, organizational structuring, rational frameworks and so on. All are meant to remove emotion from our decision-making. Yet they're all largely irrelevant to outsiders for the obvious reason that we cannot remove emotion from our decision-making. It's ingrained.

Emotion drives our decisions, even when suppressed. The best we can hope for is to put emotion in its place as just one part of our process for developing strong judgement: something renowned thinker and physician Edward de Bono espouses in a series of books, though most famously in *Six Thinking Hats* (1985).

Sometimes referred to as the 'father of lateral thinking', de Bono in *Six Thinking Hats* describes what he calls 'parallel thinking', which is his revolutionary attempt to remove bias from decision-making by, in fact, including it. Elements such as emotion, prejudice and ego have a role, he states. So by giving them an open and equal place, alongside more rational considerations, they're no longer the secret saboteurs of good decision-making. At least that's the theory.

Of course, he achieves this via his six hats, which indicate different roles in our evaluation process:

- The *white hat* represents objectivity. The focus here is on the known facts and figures in any evaluation.
- The *red hat* represents our emotions. This allows our feelings their say in our decision-making.
- The *black hat* represents caution and pessimism. What are the weaknesses and dangers and where are the threats?
- The *yellow hat* represents optimism. What are the positives and opportunities, including our best hoped-for outcome?
- The *green hat* represents creativity. The focus here is on new ideas and innovation.
- The *blue hat* represents overall control. This includes the processes and organization of decision-making, as well as how we'll ultimately come to a decision.

De Bono suggests no hard and fast rules for sequence, although it's reasonable to assume the blue hat – setting the rules and agenda – begins and ends the process, and that the white hat – dealing with the known facts – is utilized 'towards the beginning'.

He also implores us to generate balance between each hat, ensuring that 'confirmation bias' (see below) – in which we seek answers that support our prejudices (perhaps by overstating a particular hat) – is removed. In fact, given that some bias is inevitable, it should at least be recognized as a potentially-distorting concern – something that's even true of our adopted sequence.

The relevance of de Bono

For me, de Bono's methodology represents a memorable extrapolation of normal – or at least rational – decision-making. It involves no MBA-types forcing us through a complex matrix or convoluted balance scorecard. Each hat is obviously relevant and deserves consideration. Importantly, it's also applicable to individuals, while many methodologies – for instance, from Harvard Business School – are team-based so can sound ridiculous when applied to someone sitting in their bedroom on the horns of a dilemma. And it not only allows our emotions to be heard, it accepts our contradictions – another inevitable part of any human being's evaluation process.

'When two offered pieces of information disagree,' says de Bono, 'there is no argument on that point. Both pieces of information are put down in parallel. Only if it becomes essential to choose between them will the choice be made.'

Certainly, every hat has its role. While the white hat sheds light on hard facts, it also defines what information is missing and needed while offering no opinion. The red hat, meanwhile, is all about the non-rational aspects of decision-making that cannot be eradicated, though can be suppressed. It's the exact opposite of white-hat thinking – focusing instead on what gets the blood pumping and the adrenalin flowing.

Of course, the black hat's all about our darkest fears, which is something outsiders know all about.

'Black hat thinking is not balanced,' says de Bono. 'Under the black hat the brain is sensitized to check out possible danger, problems and obstacles. The focus is on why something may not work or may not be the right thing to do.'

This is balanced by the yellow hat, which is all about our sunny expectations of success. It's positive, speculative, open-minded and exploratory. And while it's not innovative (that's the green hat), it certainly involves the best outcomes for our visions and dreams.

Yes, the green hat's about growing new ideas. It's about being provocative: exploring the boundaries, pushing the envelope. It involves 'thought experiments' that cannot be predicted. Indeed, here lie the blind alleys of the (by now familiar) creative process, although de Bono also emphasizes the green hat's role in modifying, tailoring and improving existing ideas.

And that leaves the neutrality of the blue hat:
'Wearing the blue hat, we are no longer thinking about the subject,' says de Bono. 'Instead, we are thinking about the thinking needed to explore the subject.'

Of course, de Bono's methodology must be practically applicable, especially for individuals. My method is a big A4 notebook with stream-of-consciousness scribbles under the six headings – perhaps converted to an electronic format when I feel there's enough handwritten material to warrant organizing it in an attempted sequence.

Yet it still leaves me concerned that my decision-making, while stronger, remains irrational. Have I simply found a neat way of confirming my prejudices? De Bono will no doubt claim it's the blue hat's role to eradicate imbalance and prejudice, although we may have to accept that prejudice – especially emotional prejudice – is inevitable (especially for outsiders) and simply be aware of that fact.

Decision-making mistakes

In fact, reading books on decision-making – including the excellent *Decisive* (2013) by corporate motivators Chip and Dan Heath – makes me aware of my many mistakes when decision-making.

My top 10 is below:

1. *The self-fulfilling prophesy.* Sociologist Robert K. Merton identified this classic outsider outcome in 1948 – describing it as a 'false definition of the situation evoking a new behaviour which makes the originally false conception come *true*'. In decision-making, this is related to 'confirmation bias' (a 'heuristic', or rule of thumb), in which we're keen on making decisions that reinforce our prejudices or emotions. This even impacts de Bono's white-hat fact-finding: 'When people have the opportunity to collect information from the world,' write Chip and Dan Heath, 'they are more likely to

select information that supports their pre-existing attitudes, beliefs and actions'.

2. *Availability bias.* Another decision-making heuristic that harms balanced judgement – this time by making us overly concerned by what's in front of us at the expense of what's out of sight. A decision between two pitches, for instance, will favour the one delivered personally, no matter what the merits of the one delivered electronically. More recent information also wins out over something heard previously, as does something more attention-grabbing. For instance, fear of flying, as well as our expectations of winning the lottery, are examples of availability bias due to the fact air disasters and lottery wins are newsworthy events – making them appear more likely than, say, individual road deaths that barely get a mention despite their commonality.

3. *False or flawed memories*, in which logical decision-making is flawed by mistakenly assuming the circumstances match a previous – usually negative – experience. Sure, there are lessons to be learnt from our mistakes but each decision has a unique context, making concerns about repetition more an emotional barrier than a warning to be heeded. Of course, this can equally work the other way – assuming something will succeed simply because it worked previously. Yet the circumstances are unique, all of which goes to prove just how difficult good judgement can be.

4. *Assuming extreme outcomes.* This is the 'all-or-nothing' thinking typical of those with poor judgement. Most outcomes are incremental: favourable ones generating a step forward, while unfavourable ones result in a step back. Yet we tend to assume they're either life-changing or ruinous, which ups the ante and puts too much pressure on our decisions. Meanwhile, if we assume and plan for incremental results, we'd reduce both the fear and the bravado of decision-making as well as eliminate the 'false breakthroughs' mentioned in Chapter 10. Of course, the likes of Bayley and Mavity insist pitch moments can

generate leaps, as they can. But this still makes progress a linear, step-by-step process rather than the overnight rebirths we assumed. In fact, we should be wary of giant leaps – they are rarely all they seem.

5. *Restricting the outcome.* Many bad judgements come down to misunderstanding the full range of available options. Chip and Dan Heath call this the 'narrow frame', a classic mistake of the young, they state, as they too often frame questions into 'whether or not' decisions. Should they do this college course, or not, go to this party, or not. 'They see only a small slither of the spectrum of options available to them,' they write – adding that organizations, in this respect, tend to think like teenagers (as do outsiders, come to that). Their response: 'multi-tracking' in which we consider more than one option simultaneously. Creating a list of nine possible college courses – with the tenth choice a gap-year in Botswana, say – is multi-tracking, as we're deciding between positive choices. And that's certainly less terrifying than a yes/no dichotomy. That said, beware 'sham options', falsely offered to give the appearance of width.

6. *Making decisions too quickly.* 'Between stimulus and response there is a space,' wrote Viktor Frankl. 'In that space is our power to choose our response.' In other words, given time, we can choose our best reaction. Too often, we behave reactively when faced with a judgement or dilemma: coming to knee-jerk decisions that are, inevitably, overly-focused on our emotions. Yet the more time we can add to the decision-making process, the more rational our decision-making will become.

7. *Putting off decisions.* Yet the opposite is also true. Spending too long musing over decisions smacks of procrastination. Here, we may fear the outcome from execution or even from having to favour one option over another. Stuck, we condemn ourselves to a creeping paralysis in which we become incapable of judgement – a typical outsider conundrum. So there's definitely a middle way between fast and slow judgement – hence the 'six hats' formula forcing us to consider, but also encouraging us to conclude.

8. *Group-think.* Groups can make strong decisions – perhaps bringing balance to any prejudices within 'six hats' thinking. Yet groups have their own traps, the most likely of which is the desire to avoid conflict, which results in consensus-seeking (often lowest common-denominator) decisions. The other is the perceived need to generate 'fair' solutions. Certainly, I can remember both, with neither producing strong outcomes. Chip and Dan Heath suggest an alternative: a negotiated decision – basically horse-trading until all sides can live with the choice (perhaps having won on things that matter to them by conceding on points that matter more to others). And instead of fair decisions, seek 'just' decisions that are fair in terms of the process used even if some think the outcome unfair. Democracy is a classic example of a 'just' process producing, for some, unfair results. That said, group-think – at least initially – is a rare concern for alienated and contrary outsiders.

9. *Escalating sunk costs.* Again, an emotional concern: if we've previously invested time/money/emotion into something, we're more willing to invest more of the same, even once we realize it's failing to produce the desired results. Too often small failures are turned into major disasters by this 'escalation of commitment' – what's known as 'throwing good money [or anything else] after bad'. Yet anything that's been previously spent is a 'sunk cost', which is a poor justification for further spending. Of course, it's equally stupid to abandon projects at the first setback, so how can we decide what's worth further investment and what should be abandoned? The 'six hats' process, that's how – with the white hat (for facts and figures) being particularly important for informing, and perhaps altering, other-hat thinking.

10. *Superstition.* And finally there's the negative influence on rational decision-making that many, including myself, deny. Even if we avoid the extremes of, say, astrology in decision-making (the indulgence of a surprising number of world leaders) we can still find ourselves wondering whether a

particular shirt is lucky or whether 'fate' plays a hand in our decisions. It doesn't, of course, but we're frail human beings trying to navigate complex judgements with limited knowledge and, ultimately, unknowable consequences. No wonder we're tempted to recruit the Ouija board or tarot cards or even just our lucky socks. That said, I've exempted religion from 'superstition' because religious faith can provide a principles- or values-based grounding that aids strong decision-making. Asking 'what would God want us to do?' is really a depersonalized way of asking 'what do our values suggest we do?' which is, ultimately, a powerful red hat proposition.

Depersonalization – a key aspect of judgement

And talk of depersonalization brings up an important potential aid when it comes to judgement and decision-making for outsiders. A key reason our decision-making is clouded by emotion is the fact our judgements, too often, are about *us*. They're personal. And this ramps up the pressure by drilling to the core of our self-esteem. Corporate judgements are easier simply because they're about a neutral, inanimate entity. Sure, corporate failure harms our collective self-esteem but it's the corporation that's failed – a depersonalized enterprise dealing with factors often beyond its control.

This makes depersonalization a potential route for improving our judgements. Just as Frankl detached himself from appalling hardship by imagining his post-war lecturing future, so we can detach ourselves from ourselves by becoming *Me Inc.*: a company (admittedly with only one current employee) pursuing goals via entirely objective judgements. As *Me Inc.*, we're likely to get more decisions right than if we're a fearful blob of emotions, overly concerned with the humiliation of failure. Indeed, if we fail as *Me Inc.*, it's not even a failure. It's simply one project experiencing a temporary setback – something we can learn from and try again.

Given this, *Me Inc.*, clearly offers outsiders an *edge* when it comes to judgement.

> *Attributes such as creativity, strategic excellence and strong judgement can all help give outsiders that required* edge. *Yet particularly disadvantaged outsiders should be aware that any* edge *can become quickly blunted by the wrong influences, which is our concern for Part Four.*

PART FOUR
The Wrong Voices

12

AVOIDING NEGATIVITY

'There's an old joke: two elderly women are at a Catskill mountain resort and one of them says, "The food in this place is really terrible." The other one says "Yes, I know. And such small portions." Well that's essentially how I feel about life – full of loneliness and misery and suffering and unhappiness, and it's all over much too quickly.'

The Oscar-winning movie *Annie Hall* (1977), which includes the above joke in its opening monologue, exemplifies Woody Allen's ability to turn negativity and neurosis into an art form. As well as directing the movie, Allen plays the central character – the pessimistic comedian Alvy Singer – with the film's narrative centred on explaining his failed relationship with the eponymous Annie (Diane Keaton).

Of course, to the audience the reason's obvious: Alvy's view of life is just too gloomy for the insecure yet essentially cheerful Annie.

'You're incapable of enjoying life – you're like New York,' says Annie, after leaving the world's outsider capital city for the altogether sunnier climes of California, rejecting Alvy in the process.

Self-deprecation as a defence

Alvy's negativity pervades everything he says and does. It even interferes with his early dates with Annie – for instance, in a bookstore handing Annie works on death to illustrate his outlook:

'Life is divided into the horrible and the miserable,' he explains to his bemused date. 'The horrible are like terminal cases or blind people or cripples. I don't know how they get through life. . . . And the miserable is everyone else. So when you go through life you should be thankful that you're miserable because that's very lucky.'

Yet there's a darker side to Alvy's doom-laden humour – one that manifests itself through convictions of prejudice against him for being Jewish. Alvy's certain that white Anglo-Saxon Protestant Americans (or 'WASPs') dislike him for his ethnicity, despite his best friend – the distinctly WASP-like Rob (Tony Roberts) – accusing him of paranoia.

And it's here where things get interesting with respect to Woody Allen – not least because many assume that Alvy Singer's negativity is a surrogate for Allen's own neurosis. Allen – the Bronx-born son of a waiter – is clearly on display, not just in *Annie Hall* but throughout his early movies. What's more, Allen's comedy is viewed as an integral part of the self-deprecating humour typical of urban Jewish anxiety regarding their outsider status.

'The underlying message in Allen's self-deprecating humour is that, mostly because of his Jewishness, he feels like an outsider, probably because he assumes alienation is a natural part of his identity as a member of a minority,' writes academic Mark E. Bleiweiss in a chapter on Allen's Jewish humour for Charles L.P. Silet's work *The Films of Woody Allen: Critical Essays* (2006).

According to Bleiweiss, it's this sense of alienation – expressed through comic pessimism – that makes Allen's audiences so empathetic. The impression given is that, for the likes of Alvy, integration into high society is structurally impossible. Yet the opposite view is also presented through external eyes such as Annie's – who wonders whether Alvy's issues are not equally due to self-denigration. It's a position summed up by Groucho Marx's famous joke (referenced by Alvy) that he'd refuse to join any club having him as a member.

As any of my early girlfriends can attest, Alvy's pessimism certainly chimes with my own. Though not an urban Jew (if only!), I've spent most of my adult years rejecting clubs that would have me as a member. Rootless, I'd easily lapse into paranoia and negativity whenever facing major hurdles – especially those involving others I perceived as my social betters. And, yes, this could lead to the same self-denigration, of which self-deprecation – a humorous gloss that tries to own the insult (perceived or real) – was usually the most public.

For outsiders, it seems, negativity comes with the territory. Yet it's a destructive, *edge*-blunting trait, and one we must counter if our quest for meaning is to make progress.

Countering negativity using CBT

Thank heavens, then, for Albert Ellis (1913–2007), the granddaddy of psychoanalysts examining negativity and its consequences. Ellis – born into a Jewish family with a largely absent father and a bipolar mother – is credited with developing Rational Emotive Behaviour Therapy (REBT), which focuses on our reactions to experiences, as well as how these generate and perpetuate our negative 'belief systems'.

Aaron Beck and other psychologists later built upon Ellis's work to launch Cognitive Behavioural Therapy (CBT). This is a 'talking therapy' based on challenging the link between (cognitive) self-beliefs and negative (behavioural) reactions. Simple and accessible, CBT has grown into the world's most widely-applied and readily-accepted psychotherapy – helping millions overcome, though not cure, their ingrained negativity.

For Ellis and the later CBT advocates, negativity is a consequence of our reactivity. It's automatic – usually a defensive reaction to what we perceive as threats, perhaps to our safety or status. Our belief systems – developed through conditioning since birth (though some also claim a genetic inheritance) – learn to expect the worst and react defensively when that expectation is, inevitably, met.

'People and things do not upset us,' says Ellis. 'Rather we upset ourselves by believing that they can upset us.'

If we believe we're unworthy, we'll study others' behaviour for confirmation. We'll even conjure the circumstances to prove ourselves right. Of course, this becomes self-reinforcing. A lover's tiff, for those with negative self-beliefs, becomes a matter of rejection that confirms our status as an unlovable person – leaving the more emotionally-able partner wondering how a small disagreement (perhaps over a movie) so quickly descended into a relationship-threatening spat.

It's just such a spiral that REBT/CBT aims to counter. It's our evaluation of negative events that's crucial. If we can take time to consider the situation ('it's just a movie') – rather than sticking with our initial, defensive, reactions ('it's typical of her to undermine me') – we can help rationalize them. And from here we can develop a more effective, or at least less damaging, response: hopefully one that aligns our belief system with our goals rather than our fears.

Two outsiders clash

Yet this is hard work – requiring constant vigilance that's easily lost in a heated moment, as demonstrated by a recent incident of my own. While with my nine-year-old boy at a fashionable farmers' market in East London – a classic sign of the area's gentrification over recent years – my son accidently stood on the foot of a large middle-aged man. He complained. So I asked George to apologise, which he did politely – as taught by his well-educated mother.

'Do that again and I'll kill you,' the man growled in response.

My initial reaction was not to react – intending to say nothing and perhaps express surprise at such a strong response once we'd moved on. But George started crying, which hijacked my rationality. While moving away I angrily remonstrated with the man. Yet I was met with further abuse. Now triggered to a state of fury, I found my wife – who'd been buying beads in a sewing shop – deposited George, and returned.

'Say that again to my child and *I'll kill you,*' I barked.

Smiling, he offered more abuse – along the lines of leaving the area if I didn't like it – all delivered with a level and entirely-unperturbed voice as well as a 'sit on that' finger-salute. I was left with a choice: hit him or walk away. I walked away, shouting 'you're pathetic'. Inwardly, however, I knew I was the pathetic one – the angry wimp, incapable of carrying out my threats.

Having analysed the incident to a depth worthy of a Woody Allen movie, I'm finally able to offer a rational analysis. His initial response to a nine-year-old child was appalling, for sure. Yet my negative self-beliefs prevented me reacting rationally. His threat to my child made me feel unworthy – so instead of breaking the tension by, perhaps, assuming he was attempting dark humour and responding with a sardonic joke – I silently and desperately fought my internal emotional turmoil, which left George feeling abandoned. My negativity had, yet again, let me down – generating a series of self-confirming reactions.

But so had his, I now realize. I responded as the threatened small kid in a rough Essex comprehensive (such was my conditioning): first by trying to avoid the threat and then by over-reacting defensively. Yet, equally, he surely knew this was no way to address a child. My guess is that he was reacting to what he saw as an interloping middle-class family gentrifying his once edgy outsiders' enclave – with George's polite apology triggering irritation at his loss.

Two defensive outsiders, in other words, sparked into near-violent reactions by perceived threats.

Maslow and motivation

Nodding sagely at such events would have been Abraham Maslow (1908–1970). A Jewish New Yorker raised in a non-Jewish area, Maslow – along with Albert Ellis – formed part of the humanist movement within psychology. Building on existentialism, humanism focuses on the key drivers for 'normal' human behaviour such as safety, love, self-esteem and 'self-actualization' (the notion of becoming all we can be, not dissimilar to 'finding meaning').

Interestingly, Maslow's less concerned about defensive reactivity as a force for negativity than about motivation. Like Aristotle, Maslow assumes humans follow a critical path in pursuit of their goals: ones usually based on achieving self-actualization. Given this, negativity is no more than an outward expression of frustration at our poor progress towards our objectives.

This is best expressed in Maslow's famous *Hierarchy of Needs*. Here, we ascend through basic physiological requirements such as food and water all the way up to 'self-transcendence', in which our need is to 'give back' – perhaps through charity. Yet to reach this exalted level there are intermediate needs that *must* be satisfied. The caveat being that, like a computer game, we can only reach the next level having conquered the lower need.

So we'll only seek safety once no longer hungry or thirsty. Only once we're safe, perhaps via shelter, will we seek love and belonging. Only once we feel we belong, perhaps via love, can we seek self-esteem via achievement, recognition and/or material wealth. And only once we have self-esteem, can we explore self-actualizing needs such as creativity, morality and charity.

Given this, Maslow's wary eye would have settled upon the scene at the farmer's market and spotted the conflicting needs that triggered both adults' negative reactivity. My adversary perceived a challenge to his sense of belonging: the 'yuppies' arrival, having threatened his bohemian rejectionist haven, though he'd be well-advised to avoid farmers' markets in future. Yet his needs were ahead of mine, which involved dealing with perceived threats to my child's safety.

The positivity of negativity

Maslow's perspectives are certainly enlightening. Yet they're not that useful, unlike those of psychologist Julie K. Norem. Her contention is that negative thinking has a strong upside, as long as we're able to harness it to aid our need for achievement. Writing in *The Positive*

Power of Negative Thinking (2002), Norem views emotions such as anxiety not as disabling reactions but as an enabling response to unknown challenges.

Pessimists expect the worst, she says, and 'spend lots of time and energy mentally rehearsing, in vivid, daunting, detail exactly how things might go wrong'.

Of course, such anxiety looks disabling – especially in a world placing so much emphasis on positivity and confidence. Yet what she terms 'defensive pessimism' can help us work through our negative concerns, putting us in a stronger position. Rather than denying or ignoring woes, Norem claims we can instead address them – resulting in us achieving things, not *despite* our negativity, but *because* of it.

This approach certainly works for me. Denying my fears – say of public speaking – doesn't make them go away. I approach events incapable of adopting the positive 'self-talk' of CBT teachings – instead obsessing about tiny concerns: will the laptop and projector connect, will the microphone work, is my hair too long/short, will someone in the audience spot that fatal flaw I so dread, etc.?

Every concern is a real one – based on previous, usually negative, experiences. Rather than ignore these worries, however, the adoption of Norem's defensive pessimism – perhaps by listing all the worries and dealing with them one-by-one – helps me feel more in control. For instance, when accepting the gig I ask about the audience and their expectations, and tailor the talk – and my appearance – accordingly. Prior to the day, I speak to the host and go over the kit required and who'll bring it – although arrive with leads and adaptors anyway (just in case).

The result: yes, continued anxiety – to the point I'd never 'wing it' – but a growing inner confidence regarding public speaking.

Could stoicism be the answer?

But is Norem's approach *too* practical, leaving us still fretting, even if for positive ends? And how can it cope with others' clear negativity towards us, such as my man in the market? Perhaps we need an alternative to negativity. Perhaps we need stoicism: a movement founded in ancient Athens by Zeno of Citium.

Zeno taught that destructive emotions such as negativity are the result of errors in judgment that can be eradicated, he claimed, by 'moral and intellectual perfection'. Self-control and fortitude are our tools for developing this perfection, he states – allowing us to become clear thinkers capable of understanding and judgement through detached reasoning (not dissimilar to *Me Inc.* depersonalization).

A key aspect to stoicism involves virtue: i.e. improving the individual's ethical and moral well-being so that we're in agreement with nature. This means being free from 'anger, envy and jealousy' when dealing with others, as well as accepting even slaves as 'equals of other men, because all men alike are products of nature'.

Stoics accept that they're not in control of what happens, although can choose how to respond (echoing Frankl). They also accept that, if it's not possible to influence the world, it's at least possible to moderate the world's influence on them. That said, the purpose of such detachment shouldn't be contempt or even withdrawal but understanding – working out how obstacles can be converted into something useful for our purposes.

Admittedly, Zeno's teachings are a tall order for the negative outsider – wrapped up as we are in our self-assessed misfortunes and pettiness. Yet stoicism's practical outcomes look well-adjusted for the modern age, which may explain why the philosophy is going through a revival thanks to authors such as Ryan Holiday. His book, *The Obstacle is the Way: The Ancient Art of Turning Adversity to Advantage* (2014) encourages us to use adversity – including born disadvantages – as levers for our success. Just as Woody Allen made a virtue, even a career, of the alienation he perceived as a Jew – as well as his small stature and comic looks – so we can use the very elements that, we feel, go against us and turn them into strengths.

'Great individuals, like great companies,' writes Holiday, 'find a way to transform weakness into strength. They took what should have held them back – what in fact might be holding you back right this very second – and used it to move forward.'

Far from being a remote and unfashionable philosophical route to overcoming adversity, Holiday claims stoicism is the near-universal attitude adopted by those making a difference, whether they know they're exercising Zeno's teachings or not.

'As it turns out,' writes Holiday, 'this is one thing all great men and women of history have in common. Like oxygen to fire, obstacles become fuel for the blaze that was their ambition. Nothing could stop them, they were (and continue to be) impossible to discourage or contain. Every impediment only served to make the inferno within them burn with greater ferocity. These were the people who flipped their obstacles upside down.'

A riposte to Gladwell

Of course, this sounds like Gladwell's treatise extolling the advantages of the disadvantaged, which is where we came in. In fact, it's the perfect riposte. Gladwell erroneously assumes successful outsiders (or 'misfits' as he calls them) are leveraging *advantages* that simply looked like disadvantages – a skewed view that inspired this book. In reality, according to Holiday, Zeno, Marcus Aurelius and many other known stoics, successful outsiders are leveraging genuine *disadvantages* to give them the grit, the resilience – and, yes, the *edge* – to succeed *anyway*.

Such disadvantages, if viewed stoically, turn out to be useful – even if, as with my educationally-limiting Essex background, their only use is to authenticate the struggle. In fact, forget Essex – five minutes spent viewing the Paralympic Games should be enough to prove the power of stoicism. These are real disadvantages – not advantages in disguise (as Gladwell claims). They're just being employed in order to find meaning, something Viktor Frankl would surely applaud.

Holiday's book has become a bestseller among Silicon Valley entrepreneurs, with stoicism becoming a byword for the resilience required to succeed in such a ferociously competitive environment. Among the testosterone-fuelled intensity of the digital economy, the stoic watchwords involve mastering emotions, keeping heads, retaining perspective and viewing challenges as opportunities: all helping those companies – often founded by contrarian outsiders – forge an *edge*.

A 10-point plan for adopting stoicism

1. *Don't be intimidated by others.* Epictetus (a Roman stoic, though one born into slavery) advised us to imagine others having sex as a way of bringing them down to earth. That said, negative people could twist that into an attack on their own self-esteem, so how about picturing others on the toilet – the image that reduces us all to our most vulnerable?
2. *Remove flummery and ornamentation* – and discard euphemism. Yes, it's the 'toilet', not the 'bathroom' and meat's just a dead animal: both wonderfully liberating thoughts for the cynic. Meanwhile, ceremonies filled with icons and embellishment – usually conspired that way to generate awe – look pretty unimpressive with the nonsense removed.
3. *Realize rude people are underestimating you*, which is to your advantage. They're also being honest, which can be useful. In fact, beware flatterers – they're usually the ones trying to take advantage.
4. *You're on your own.* Don't expect others to help or save you: they won't. Indeed, be wary of 'saviours'. Instead, develop fortitude, persistence and pragmatism.
5. *Don't waste time.* Your rivals are working hard while you're on the beach or in the pub, so ensure that your time's well spent.
6. *Be creative with problems* – seeing them as strong opportunities. Even a lost client or failed pitch or post-interview rejection offers the chance to learn and the space to hone your skills and/ or change direction.

7. *Forget false positivity and optimism* – they're emotional positions, no different to negativity and pessimism. Instead, be creative and look for practical opportunities.

8. *If necessary, lie to yourself.* Setbacks are simply those judged to be so. But you don't have to agree. Decide your own narrative, even if others think you a fantasist.

9. *Nervousness is an indulgence,* usually caused by doubt. So never 'wing it' – do the work required to ensure you're on top of your brief. After all, that's what your rivals are doing.

10. *Emotions act as barriers to a solution* – making you indulge in the problem rather than think and act in ways that generate the solution. So the sooner your emotions can be brought under control, the sooner your weaknesses can become your strengths.

13

THE DANGER OF EXTREMISM

On 5 November 1605, a plot led by Robert Catesby – and including the explosives expert Guy Fawkes – succeeded in blowing up the English Parliament, killing scores of statesmen as well as King James I of England (VI of Scotland). Yet the atrocity failed in its central aim of instigating a Catholic insurrection against the Protestant crown. Instead, it sparked a backlash against Catholicism that destroyed England's nascent tolerance of private religious conviction.

The conspirators and anyone associated with them were butchered – as were many senior Catholics holding high office (having sworn an 'oath of supremacy'). In every town, 'recusants' (as Catholics were known) were burnt out of their homes as a bloody pogrom ensued. For generations, a firebrand Puritanism held sway throughout an England despised abroad for its Protestant extremism – in fact, admired only for its many talented exiles. . . .

Well, not quite. As many in the English-speaking world celebrate each November, the plot was uncovered and foiled. Fawkes was found along with 36 barrels of gunpowder thanks to a Catholic loyalist nobleman who'd been tipped off to avoid Parliament. Catesby and other conspirators fled London, only to be gunned down in a shoot-out worthy of a Hollywood western. Fawkes and the remaining conspirators were tortured, tried and executed.

And while the plotters themselves were brutally dispatched, the cause of religious tolerance ambled on. Catholics willing to swear somewhat bolstered oaths – and not advertise their faith – retained high-office and were soon joined by others. Indeed, Catholicism itself was gradually accommodated, while England continued its meandering path towards religious freedom: by the 1720s becoming what exiled French enlightenment philosopher Voltaire described as the land of '60 religions and only one sauce' (gravy).

Radicalism and the outsider

Of course, this is a somewhat romanticized view of English history, and one many Catholics may take issue with (official discrimination against Catholicism lasted into the nineteenth century, after all, and is even today off-limits with respect to the monarchy). Yet its broad truth – along with my guess at the likely outcome had Fawkes lit the fuse – serves to illustrate one of the most disabling traits for outsiders in search of meaning: extremism. As outsiders, we're prone to becoming radicalized, a trait that – while potentially offering an *edge* in terms of creativity and even entrepreneurialism – is, in wider society, a disaster.

Extremism feeds on itself – using anger at perceived (or real) injustice to further fuel initially-genuine feelings of alienation. Far from being insightful, extremists develop a blinkered vision that blocks out anything not supporting their narrow view. If unresolved, extremists eventually lose sight of reality – even leveraging off the indifference and ridicule of the moderate majority. Violence – including terrorism – can follow.

'Terrorists try to force the world to meet their narcissistic, grandiose, demands, and when this doesn't happen, they lash out violently,' writes psychologist Stephen A. Diamond, author of *Anger, Madness, and the Daimonic: The Psychological Genesis of Violence, Evil and Creativity* (1999).

In different ways, both Catesby and Fawkes fit this mould. Catesby was a provincial from Warwickshire, born the third son of a prominent Catholic family. He grew into a tall, charming, persuasive, yet egotistic and neurotic gentleman. He became embittered by the mistreatment of some prominent Catholics under Elizabeth I – even joining a failed rebellion in 1601. This resulted in a brief stint in prison: a benign outcome for the era though one that inflamed his rage. And after the 'false breakthrough' of King James's accession in 1603, this became a seething quest for revenge.

As a man with a Catholic mother and wife, James Stuart offered hope for those wanting England to return to the 'true religion'. And the fact James, instead, reinforced the relatively tepid anti-Catholic laws disappointed prominent Catholics and infuriated young hotheads such as Catesby. Soon, they were outbidding each other with their violent fantasies – lurid revolutionary dreams that would have remained so, had it not been for Guy Fawkes.

Interestingly, Fawkes was born to a prominent Protestant family – stalwarts of York society, no less. That said, his mother's side, the Jacksons, were listed as recusants – an influence that began to exert itself after his father's death when Guy was just eight. Fawkes attended St Peter's, a known (if nominally loyal) Catholic school, where his identity confusion – mixed with the school's underlying sense of resentment – turned him into an extremist: a common response for outsiders among the alienated.

Dismissed from his first employment – revealingly, to a nobleman due to attend Parliament that day – Fawkes left England to serve the Catholic cause in the Spanish military. Here, he became radicalized beyond redemption – changing his name to *Guido* and gaining rapid promotions while developing a strong reputation as the go-to man for explosions. Indeed, he was employing his exothermic skills against the Protestants of Holland when Catesby's men caught up with him with promises of power and glory.

Fawkes thus joined the plot as a battle-hardened fighter, as well as an expert in gunpowder. Catesby's charisma and bravado was now fatally matched by Fawkes's knowledge and experience – and the extremist fantasies of both fused into plans and actions.

Terrorism's infantile and narcissistic roots

Of course, the Gunpowder Plot has fascinated historians down the centuries. Yet its purpose here is to illustrate how extremism, even terrorism, emerges as an option within the minds of young and alienated outsiders. Usually due to childhood experiences, many develop sometimes self-fulfilling (though often justifiable) convictions of persecution that – in early adulthood – gel into a burning sense of injustice. A revolutionary zeal embeds itself: turning anger into fury that concocts a desperate need for vengeance. Few – thankfully – possess the will to execute their bloody fantasies and fewer still the organizational or technical skills to pull them off. For those with both, infamy and immortality awaits – hence the attraction.

The biographies of some of recent history's most notorious terrorists – from Osama bin Laden, to Anders Behring Breivik, Timothy McVeigh and even the 'Unabomber' Ted Kaczynski – all reveal strong signs of alienation, usually through their family situation. As we saw in Part One, this leads to embattled identities and a psychological immaturity that can fuel anger, resentment, hatred and rage. The result: vengeful atrocities and personal catastrophe – meaning that, whatever the temptations (in terms of notoriety), extremism is a selfish and pathetic use of an outsiders' potential.

It's also entirely unnecessary.

'Terrorism is a failure to find a creative solution to life, to finding and fulfilling one's true destiny,' writes Diamond.

Interestingly, many terrorists – while outsiders – are far from disadvantaged. As we've seen, both Catesby and Fawkes were high born, as was *Al-Qaeda's* founder Osama bin Laden – the seventeenth child of billionaire Mohammed bin Awad bin Laden. As with Fawkes, Osama's father died while he was a boy, leaving him rich, bored and looking for meaning. This he found aged 22 when the Soviets invaded Afghanistan – his financial and physical support to the ultimately-victorious *mujahideen* providing the sense of purpose bin Laden so craved.

A seductive proposition

Of course, bin Laden's destructive capabilities, although eventually fatal, seem attractive to many outsiders because they're so powerful. Directly and indirectly, he's generated wars, invasions, atrocities and deaths by the thousand. His deeds have infuriated superpowers and his legacy inspires millions – creating a private army of recruits willing to sacrifice their lives for the cause he articulated through his actions.

Yet such radicalism's a lie: one that ruins the lives of disadvantaged outsiders. The advantaged persuade them to don the warrior headband and sacrifice their lives inflating someone else's ego. Bin Laden's family wealth wasn't a coincidental aspect of his leadership and notoriety. *It was the cause of it.* It gave him the money and organizational skills required, as well as the confidence to recruit. For the enlisted foot soldiers, however, the false promises of glory are followed by an anonymous death that satisfies no one other than the exaggerated vanity of their narcissistic leaders.

And it's not just terrorism that follows this abusive trajectory. Nearly all forms of extremism share the same characteristics: advantaged outsiders recruiting the genuinely alienated as cannon fodder for their egotistic quests. Whether Lenin, Mao Tse-tung, Che Guevara or Fidel Castro – it's nearly always the well-off and well-educated rabble-rousers that enlist the less-advantaged to do their often-violent bidding.

As an outcome, it's one I detest because, yet again, the disadvantaged have been manipulated by the advantaged.

Blind to realities

That said, those in the throes of extremism find this an impossible message to absorb – something reaffirmed for me during the 2009 anti-capitalist protests in the City of London (coinciding with the G20 summit). Thanks to the power of social media I became embroiled in a debate with one of the protests' self-declared leaders. He'd been arrested – a proud moment for this latter-day Che Guevara, busy rallying the downtrodden and leading the charge against the capitalist oppressor. Of course, I saw his role differently, although I was in part slaking my irritation at the protest, which had resulted in a cancelled pitch meeting (so apologies for the initial sarcasm).

The exchange went something like this (edited for brevity):

RK (me): Come on kiddies, you've had your fun? Great day out. Now back to your studies.

AP (him): It's the state's response that's childish. They send thuggish policeman to protect banks full of millionaires from the poor and disenfranchised. Someone has to fight back against the obscene inequalities of an unfair and destructive system that wrecks lives for the vast majority of ordinary people. If you can't see how appallingly corrupt that is then you're fooling yourself. At least my eyes are open.

RK: Your eyes are open to what you want to see. The situation you describe is one extremists have manufactured to appear that way. Provocateurs act threateningly and the police have to protect those inside. They'd have protected a hospital or even the Communist Party headquarters the same way.

AP: Extremists? Provocateurs? I guess that's me you're talking about. Yet the only 'provocateurs' were the police, using batons against the innocent. And the extremists are those inside the banks fleecing the poor to enrich themselves. As I say, open your eyes.

RK: That's one way of looking at it. I disagree but I'll not focus on converting you – I'm just worried your anger has generated a radicalism within you that's wasted. It's pointless. It's also being manipulated by others. If you're on the front line being arrested, you're no leader. You're a lieutenant at best – cannon fodder. Who's controlling you?

AP: I'm being manipulated? I'm controlled? You really have taken the shilling haven't you? I'm just doing something about a system that shuts out the vast majority. I'm trying to build a world based on justice and sustainability. What do you want? More crap for your attic and to hell with the planet? It's not me being manipulated mate.

RK: Maybe. Perhaps we're both seeing what we want to see, having been fed various 'truths'. Maybe we're both pawns of 'their' propaganda. Yet mine doesn't end on the barricades or being arrested. I end up with my own company and a sense of fulfilment. Sure, there are frustrations and inequities – and some have it easier than others. But it has a future. Your future is based on ideology, and rioting when your unrealistic dreams don't materialize. Sure, it's fun, but it ultimately goes nowhere. It's a waste of a good mind.

AP: Someone has to say 'no more'. Someone has to fight back. Someone has to point out the hypocrisy. I'd rather live honestly – true to myself – than die a fat, smug, consumer of STUFF made through exploitation. And you make it sound like I'm alone. There were thousands on that protest, and hundreds of thousands – if not millions – on protests like it around the world.

RK: Of those on that protest 90 percent will go back to their studies, graduate, get a job and join the 'system' you so despise. Of the remaining 10 percent, nearly all will end up embittered losers – having wasted their talents and potential on impossible ideologies. That leaves a tiny fraction – probably just one among the thousands on your protest – who'll become the intellectual leader you fancy yourself to be. They'll address rallies, write books, gain notoriety and potentially win fame. Great, except they'll almost certainly have had an expensive education and the connections and confidence to get themselves noticed. Hope that's you. If not, my guess is you'll get a low return for that criminal record.

AP: Don't force your hierarchical obsession on me. Come and meet us, we're ordinary people – just sick of the lies and destruction . . .

And on it went: me telling him he'll see 'ordinary people' at Liverpool Street Station during weekday rush-hours, all bettering themselves through diligence; him saying I'd built my 'false consciousness' on the back of others' efforts that wrecked lives and destroyed eco-systems.

An enabling romanticism

Did I win? Absolutely not. Yet my issue was not with his politics – the system discriminates, for sure – but with the outcome. He was following an existentialist tradition going back to Sartre, Nietzsche and even Kierkegaard. He'd analysed the human experience, found it wanting, and was making a stand against its inequities. So far, so outsider.

He was doing himself no favours, however, because he was not in a position of power – making him no more than a foot-soldier for the advantaged. His rage boiled over into illegal action because that was its only outlet – hence his arrest: the usual result (other than death) for the disadvantaged making a stand.

Sure, my view of the Liverpool Street commuters could, again, be described as romantic. But it's an enabling romanticism – affording me a psychological advantage over him, whether I had the political upper hand or not. For a start, I'd been him: the angry young man railing against 'the system' – even experiencing what I saw as police brutality during the 1990 Poll Tax riot in Trafalgar Square.

Yet I'd since experienced many years watching ordinary people make progress through work – prospering in structures that looked iniquitous to the lowly but are, in fact, highly meritocratic. At the very least they offer skills that can be used for personal gain – helping give us an *edge* – even if we have to become entrepreneurs to utilize them meaningfully. Despite myself, this even included me, although I had to start my own business to get beyond my outsider convictions – not an untypical route, as we've seen. Yet I found my place in a 'system' that can accommodate even those that dislike or disagree with it, though not those actively plotting to destroy it.

As for the extremists, well it's worth noting that they usually bring about results that, while suiting their leaders, are often the reverse of what the activists had wanted. My fictional outcome for a successful Gunpowder Plot ended, not with a Catholic victory or even the gradualism of English history, but with the violent oppression of Catholicism. Of course, I made it up. But history's littered with examples of radicals engineering an exaggerated version of the injustice they railed against. Sure, it adds to the rebel-leader's power (and bolsters recruitment), but it's hardly what their supporters had hoped for. Even when successful, revolutions nearly always result in the betrayal of those that fought so hard to affect change – as Orwell so eloquently illustrated in *Animal Farm*.

Dealing with prejudice

But what about prejudice? Under *apartheid*, the black majority in South Africa was structurally excluded due to legally-sanctioned racism. The same was true in the southern USA until the 1960s – restricting the black population to the economic margins and making any attempt to forge an *edge* impossible. And while this was openly the case in those two examples, to say it's not still covertly the case – at least to some degree – in the entire western world is at best naïve and at worst blind ignorance.

And race is simply the most obvious differentiator. Gender, class, age, sexuality – even the residues of religious bigotry – all still hamper those trying to prosper as individuals judged on their merits, with well-meaning laws trying to prevent such abuse often compounding the problem. Given this, surely feelings of prejudice against us are so powerful – and, for the outsider, so ingrained – extremist responses are understandable, even acceptable?

Well, yes, they're understandable. But the question remains: are they enabling? Those you perceive as bigots (however constructed) could be the gatekeepers to your future, meaning you *must* persuade them or remain out in the cold. This poses a dilemma – and one that no self-help text can easily overcome. Yet we shouldn't surrender. If *their* prejudice is the problem, we should tackle it – perhaps not head-on, but through changes in *our* attitude that are at least enabling rather than disabling.

For instance, class is a subtle but highly-toxic prejudice – especially (though not exclusively) in Britain – resulting in my being belittled, too often, as the badly-educated 'Essex boy' among the privately-educated elite. Of course, I hate it. But I've developed my own way of preventing prejudice from derailing my progress. Below are my tips, although I add the caveat that our immediate, emotional, responses when facing prejudice can derail any of these suggestions:

1. *Pick your battles.* The fight against prejudice is to be applauded. Yet it's what Stephen Covey (of *The Seven Habits* . . . fame) calls our 'circle of concern' rather than our 'circle of influence'. Single-handedly, we cannot change the world, so we must focus on what we *can* influence – remembering that our aim is to make progress towards *our* goals.
2. *Stay mentally strong.* Remember Eleanor Roosevelt's famous quote: 'no one can make you feel inferior without your consent'. Sure, this is easy to say, but less easy to adopt. But we should say it anyway.
3. *Set your goals.* Perceptions of prejudice are often triggered by situations that make us nervous: pitches, interviews, social occasions, networking events, etc. Yet our nerves can make us overly sensitive. So we should adopt *Me Inc.*, depersonalization by calculating what we want from any situation and by focusing purely on that outcome. Everything else is just noise.
4. *Judge everything by your long-term goals.* Are these being advanced by this interaction? If not – and you sense bigotry – why hang around for the belittling? That said, you shouldn't bail until you've explored *all* the options for making progress.
5. *Dress well.* If you're trying to be provocative – fine, dress eccentrically. But it's then a tad unfair to blame others for pre-judging you on your appearance. Otherwise, dress to signal tribal acceptance, although why not be the best-dressed among them?

6. *Prepare an opening line.* This should be a positive but not boastful description that states firmly your legitimacy. Err on the side of modesty, especially in the UK, although beware self-deprecation: given their prejudices, it may be taken literally.

7. *Smile.* Even if you're as nervous as hell and hating every minute, fake it. Sporting a scowl confirms their worst suspicions, while seeing a smiling face makes everyone assume you're 'happy within yourself' and worth knowing.

8. *Put people at their ease.* There's a chance that what you perceive as their prejudice is in fact nervousness at meeting someone 'different'. So take the initiative and be interested in them. Could it be their insecurities making them seem offish? Assuming so is incredibly enabling.

9. *Seek allies.* Prejudice can feel isolating. Yet anyone perceiving prejudice is unlikely to be alone, so seek out others that may be feeling the same way. Yet don't seek to recruit them – just establish an unstated bond through neutral conversation.

10. *And finally, develop a kinder view.* All prejudice is ignorance after all, and they'll have their own worries and hierarchies to deal with. Given this, imagine your power when their bile and bigotry is met with your kindness and compliments.

14
UTILIZING (CONSTRUCTIVE) SOCIOPATHY

"Sexist, even potentially misogynist'. That was the considered opinion of some commentators with respect to my first attempt at 'finding meaning' through creativity: in this case my ill-advised foray into 'lad-lit' authoring. Even sympathetic readers – such as my mother – suggested the tone was somewhat disrespectful to the women I encountered while on the New York dating scene. An accusation that, frankly, amazed me.

From my perspective, the book was, in part, an account of my late-onset confidence when dealing with the opposite sex. The joke, I assumed, was on me: the hapless male, finally gaining a modicum of aptitude while navigating the complex codes governing the singles' scene in uptight 1990s Manhattan.

It was, I thought, a witty treatise against the enforced sexual repression of a dating culture then dominated by *The Rules* – a popular book informing women of the 'time-tested secrets of capturing the heart of Mr Right'. For other – especially female – readers, however, my book was an insulting diatribe aimed at excusing this particular male's appallingly predatory behaviour.

An exercise in sociopathy

Now married with children, I concede: it was inappropriate. That said, our post-Jimmy Savile era has somewhat hardened the frivolous and self-deprecating language – making it sound more contemptuous and antagonistic than intended. Both I and society have changed, although I apologise to anyone offended by a book that, even at its most innocent, celebrated poor sexual etiquette.

Yet both my behaviour in New York, as well as the book's publication, reveal something else about me. That I am (or at least was) a sociopath. While names were changed and identities disguised, I nonetheless demonstrated a total disregard for the people whose sensibilities I trampled. I had no conscience with respect to both my actions – piling infidelities upon infidelities, with being caught my only concern – and my desire to publish, in all its gory detail, my sexual adventures as a single Englishman in New York.

'Imagine – if you can – not having a conscience, none at all,' writes Martha Stout, psychologist and leading authority on sociopaths in *The Sociopath Next Door* (2005). 'No feelings of guilt or remorse no matter what you do, no limiting sense of concern for the well-being of strangers, friends, or even family members. Imagine no struggles with shame . . . no matter what kind of selfish, lazy, harmful, or immoral action you had taken.'

According to Stout (and others), sociopathic traits include:

- *Lack of shame*. There's no conscience or empathy, or even guilt. Sociopaths are, quite literally, shameless. Their actions are limited only by concerns regarding the personal consequences of getting caught.
- *An oversized ego*, resulting in such an enormous sense of ambition that sociopaths often feel the need to conceal it, which makes them proficient at . . .
- *Lying and manipulation*. Sociopaths are pathological liars, that are capable of lying to themselves in order to maintain the façade required to execute their objectives.
- *Charm*. Sociopaths are experts at blending in. They can exhibit high levels of superficial charm – knowing exactly what to say and how to say it in order to further their objectives.

- *Extreme individualism.* Blending in or otherwise, most socio-paths are outsiders, often with few friends and harbouring highly-individualistic attitudes towards others and society as a whole. Team players they ain't.

'It is not that this group fails to grasp the difference between good and bad,' writes Stout, 'it is that the distinction fails to limit their behaviour. The intellectual difference between right and wrong does not bring on the emotional sirens and flashing blue lights . . . that it does for the rest of us.'

Sociopathic roots

According to Stout, sociopathic tendencies are apparent in – give-or-take – one in every 25 individuals. This means that 'without the slightest blip of guilt or remorse, *one in 25 people can do anything at all*' (Stout's italics).

Uncomfortable as it is to admit, that 4 percent – at least while I lived in New York – included me. That said, confessing a sociopathic past is an odd place to find myself. Far from being too egotistic, and that being the root cause of this out-of-control Lothario, I'd spent most of my adulthood seriously under-confident, especially in my dealings with the opposite sex. In fact, I assumed nearly all women found me unattractive.

All too aware of my short stature (I'm 5'8') and awkward manner (pseudo-intellectuals are poorly-received in Essex), my youthful assumptions included the near-certainty that any romantic approach I initiated would result in rejection. Of course, this all changed in New York, although the roots of my behaviour remained embedded within my deeply-ingrained self-esteem issues.

Contemptuously, in New York I became aware that many women appreciate both male confidence (which I'd learnt to fake) and a sophisticated-sounding foreign accent. Meanwhile, I was 3,000 miles from home, so the consequences of my behaviour didn't figure, as they didn't when I saw the same behaviours as an exploitable opportunity to fulfil my, thus far frustrated, literary ambitions.

Constructive sociopathy

Yet sociopathy poses a dilemma for any outsider trying to forge an *edge*: one obvious to anyone noticing that both my core objectives – to become sexually successful and to publish a book – were achieved, not despite but *because* of my poor behaviour. Sociopathy is a highly-enabling trait, and one capable of ignoring societal obligations that may limit our success. In fact, far from being among the warnings for outsiders, shouldn't sociopathy be part of our toolbox for forging that *edge*?

Even Stout appears to share misgivings in this respect:

'Can we say for sure that sociopathy does not work for the individual who has it?' she asks. 'Is sociopathy a disorder at all, or is it functional?'

If my book had succeeded – perhaps launching my career as a renowned lad-lit writer in the Nick Hornby mould – surely I'd now view it as, indeed, highly functional? What's more, couldn't my current remorse be nothing more than a constructive way of consolidating new ambitions – perhaps allowing me to close the door on that 'failure' in order, as an unreformed sociopath, to further my career as a self-help writer? Am I still a sociopath, in other words, just presenting myself as an honest straightforward-kinda-guy wanting to help others?

In fact, yes. Correctly channelled, sociopathy *can* work in our favour. Ambition for ambition's sake – to become famous or rich or powerful – turns us into pathological (i.e. compulsive) sociopaths: with no proportionality or boundaries and with purely selfish aims. Yet properly channelled, the single-minded ambition of the sociopath is, indeed, functional. That said, the channelling's all-important.

For instance, my current ambition is to consolidate my success as a self-help writer. My sociopathic tendencies therefore allow me to explore shamelessly my past and current personal failings to illustrate important points for my books. This includes embarrassing facts about my upbringing that my immediate family would rather I didn't reveal, as well as excruciating confessions about my state of mind at various points in my life. I have no conscience about this, and feel no guilt or remorse when my mother, sister or wife complain. It's for a greater cause, albeit a selfish one.

Yet – importantly – my cause helps people, something I genuinely want to do because helping others helps me succeed as a self-help writer. My ambitions are therefore aligned with a societal good, which – within limits – allows me to explore sociopathic means for positive ends. That's not me pretending I'm a saintly person dedicated to others' needs. I'm not: in outlook, I remain closer to Rasputin than Mother Theresa (although the latter's sociopathic tendencies were apparent to writers such as Christopher Hitchens). It's just that my own needs are now correctly channelled to coincide with those I help. And that's more functional than pursuing goals that alienate people, and therefore inevitably go nowhere.

I'm not being manipulative. I'm being constructively sociopathic.

Hare's psychopath checklist

Yet dangers remain, probably the most significant of which is the need for proportionality – for boundaries – when channelling socio-pathy. If we remain unaware – perhaps no longer concerned even about the personal consequences of our actions – we're in danger of going beyond sociopathy. In fact, we're potentially entering the realm of the psychopath.

Psychopathy is a mental disorder characterized by bold antisocial behaviour, a lack of remorse and a limited concern regarding personal safety. It's also a condition receiving lots of attention lately thanks to books such as Jon Ronson's *The Psychopath Test* (2011). Actually, the test is Robert D. Hare's. As professor of psychology at the University of British Columbia, Hare developed an inventory of 20 traits (known as the *PCL-R* checklist) that denote psychopathic tendencies. Tested individuals are given scores between zero (showing no elements of a characteristic) and two (showing 'full application').

And while Hare has become concerned that the test can be over-applied, over-simplified or misread – for instance, not all the factors carry the same weight – we can assume that those scoring highly against a number of the following traits may start considering themselves psychopathic to some degree.

- Glib and superficial charm
- Grandiosity/overblown self-worth
- Need for stimulation
- Pathological lying
- Cunning and manipulation
- Lack of remorse or guilt
- Callousness/lack of empathy
- Poor behavioural controls
- Impulsiveness
- Irresponsibility
- Denial (of poor behaviour)
- Parasitic lifestyle
- Sexual promiscuity
- Early behavioural problems
- Lack of realistic long-term goals
- Failure to accept responsibility for own actions
- Many short-term marital-type relationships
- Juvenile delinquency
- Revocation of conditional release
- Criminal versatility.

Of course, many of these traits vary from sociopathic behaviour by little more than degrees. That said – and with the caveat this remains an area of fierce professional debate – the dominant trait of the sociopath appears to be their lack of conscience, while the dominant trait of the psychopath appears to be social deviancy. Psychopaths are prepared to indulge in extreme actions without regard for the consequences, an extremity that may even prevent them determining right from wrong – a divide sociopaths can determine, though often ignore.

The psychopath's advantage?

Yet the dilemma's repeated. In fact, it's underlined: are such traits so bad for ambitious outsiders in search of an *edge*? Sure, psychopaths may be less cautious and more prone to violent conduct than sociopaths, and thus more likely to be curtailed. But are the traits in themselves – again – not largely beneficial for an ambitious outsider who may, after all, have been rejected by the group?

Indeed, many people tick off the traits, not with concern, but with a sneaky glee that they may have what it takes to graduate from Hare's *Finishing School for Psychopaths*. This is a phenomenon I witnessed first-hand at a book event hosted by renowned psycho-path-studier Dr. Kevin Dutton, co-author of *The Good Psychopath's Guide to Success* (2014). He'd brought along his fellow author and self-confessed psychopath Andy McNab (also author of *Bravo Two Zero* and other true-life SAS thrillers) and, together, they subjected the audience to a psychopath test not dissimilar to Hare's checklist.

I was at the *Ivy Club* – the fashionable inner lair of ambitious London creatives – so I guess the audience's delight should have been expected. Yet, from a crowd of around 100, the test eventually selected four individuals revealing psychopathic characteristics, one severely – interestingly aligning with Stout's ratio for sociopathy, as well as the accepted clinical view that around 1 percent of the population are psychopaths to some degree.

Far from being horrified, however, the outed psychopath – an aging flamboyant male – was thrilled. And he immediately gained an aura of power over the rest of us. The other three (all female) were also clearly pleased – becoming emboldened by the charge while the rest of us looked on jealously. As negative traits go, therefore, being either sociopathic or psychopathic clearly offers some advantages for the ambitious.

Thatcher: the psychopath?

Or does it? Many historical figures have been accused of being psychopaths – and of using their mental malady as a means for winning, retaining and extending their power. Former UK prime minister Margaret Thatcher (1925–2013) is among them, perhaps unfairly for a leader three-times democratically elected and who had to fight ingrained sexism within her own party to become leader: both achievements requiring high levels of coalition-building and cooperation, one would have thought.

Thatcher was undoubtedly an outsider, although this was not solely due to her gender. She rose through the ranks of a Conservative Party dominated by aristocratic grandees that assumed their elevation a birthright. They happily intrigued against each other as part of a 'great game', though were astonished when bested by a state-educated, lower-middle class woman from small-town Lincolnshire.

The youngest daughter of a greengrocer, Thatcher came out of the blue to not only lead her party but transform it: eventually also transforming Britain, Europe, much of the former Communist world and capitalism itself. To this day, those that both love and loathe her evoke her name as a totem of what's hated/needed about society – making her probably the most transformative global politician of her age as well as someone that divides opinion in the British Isles more forcefully than any figure since Oliver Cromwell (another leader with strong outsider credentials).

Yet, according to some leading psychologists, Thatcher was also a psychopath. Or, at least, she revealed psychopathic tendencies. Sure, she could build alliances when she needed them, even in government – with the so-called 'wets' in her early Cabinets, for instance – but, ultimately, she was capable of not only making, but also relishing, blood-curdling decisions that harmed and even took countless lives. Of course, all leaders must be prepared to do the same – it's part of their *edge*. But listen to Thatcher on society . . .

'There is no such thing as society. There are individual men and women, and there are families. And no government can do anything except through people, and people must look to themselves first' . . .

. . . or this on the unions: 'We had to fight the enemy without in the Falklands. We always have to be aware of the enemy within, which is much more difficult to fight and more dangerous to liberty' . . .

. . . or even this on her own Cabinet: 'I don't mind how much my ministers talk, as long as they do what I say'.

She refused to conform to protocol – hence rubbing the Queen up the wrong way. She delighted in rocking any boat she thought needed rocking. And, ultimately, she viewed everyone as either someone likely to do her bidding – 'one of us' as she called the non-aristocratic Tories – or an enemy to be vanquished.

Thatcher's psychopathic tendencies got her to the top. But they ultimately harmed both her career and her reputation. For instance, here's her talking about those same Cabinet colleagues after they'd advised her she'd lose a second-round leadership contest against Michael Heseltine, bringing an end to her tenure as PM:

'It was treachery with a smile on its face. Perhaps that was the worst thing of all.'

In fact, it was mostly well-meant advice from allies trying to save her from a humiliating defeat that would have destroyed her legacy. But – after 11 years at the helm and 15 as Tory leader – those psychopathic tendencies wrecked her judgement and fuelled her paranoia, a not untypical end for a powerful psychopath.

Generating enmity – the psychopath's fate

Make no mistake, Thatcher was a conviction politician of the highest order – convictions that hardened in office: a countenance only a borderline-psychopath could maintain in modern democratic politics with its compromises, deals and coalitions. It was a rare feat, though one nearly repeated during Tony Blair's government, at least with respect to his foreign adventures. Without the transformative results, however, Blair's achievements pale in comparison – resulting in him being reviled by both his opponents and his erstwhile supporters.

Far from encouraging emulation – as is tempting given their cumulative 21 years in the top job – both Thatcher and Blair should therefore act as a warning for outsiders with a sociopathic or even psychopathic need for success. Both were ultimately destroyed by such tendencies because they saw the world in black and white terms. They became incapable of heeding external advice – picking fights with anyone seeing things differently and coming to view their role in near-messianic terms.

Eventually psychopaths – having run out of external enemies – start devouring their inner circle and even their closest allies. No longer building alliances to support their powerbase they, instead, generate pools of resentment and enmity until – with armies ranged against them – the knife's wielded by their closest allies. ('*Et tu, Brute?*' indeed.)

The power of synergizing

To gain that all-important *edge*, ambitious outsiders don't need to surrender their selfish ambitions, however. And they certainly don't need to become sociopaths or psychopaths. They need to 'synergize' – another of Stephen Covey's *Seven Habits* . . .

'Simply defined, [synergy] means that the whole is greater than the sum of the parts,' writes Covey. 'It means that the relationship which the parts have to each other is a part in and of itself.'

Immediately, we can see the mistake of the psycho/sociopath. Their ego prevents them recognizing the role of others in their own success, leaving them isolated and eventually brought down by their hubris – the forces ranged against them always too powerful for a single person to overcome (as even Julius Caesar discovered). Synergize, meanwhile, and the foundations become far stronger, a notion Covey claims is part of nature.

'If you plant two plants close together,' he writes, 'the roots commingle and improve the quality of the soil so that both plants will grow better than if they are separated.'

Synergizing is about looking at the world as a place where cooperation is not viewed as a compromise but as something more powerful than selfishness. It seeks not power for power's sake, but alliances built on reciprocal trust and communication. This generates unbreakable bonds, creating win–win outcomes that eclipse the potential from isolating win–lose battles (the typical zero-sum view of the psycho/sociopath).

'Synergy means that 1+1 may equal 8, 16 or even 1,600,' writes Covey. 'The synergistic position of high trust produces solutions better than any originally proposed.'

Of course, this can feel naïve: the thinking of a fool being manipulated by psycho/sociopaths perhaps. *So what!* would be Covey's response: it's still a stronger position than distrust and non-cooperation, which will quickly reduce our options. That said, Covey did allow for a 'no deal' response, perhaps when dealing with proven abusers of our trust. Yet this should not embitter us, and certainly not prevent us seeking other synergistic relationships.

Synergizing doesn't destroy individuality – it complements it, adding the dynamo of others' capabilities to our own burgeoning *edge*. Yet – if we're sociopathic, meaning we're incapable of being trustworthy – well, we should remember that one day, some day, it'll come back to bite us: probably at the very moment we most need others' help.

> *While sociopathy can give outsiders an* edge, *it will only be sustainable if it involves a constructive rather than harmful objective. And that invariably involves synergizing with others. Yet outsiders should celebrate being unrepentant individualists, not least because of their extraordinary vantage point . . .*

CONCLUSION
AN EXTRAORDINARY VANTAGE POINT

'I went to the pub. They were all singing . . . oh, some song they'd learnt from the jukebox. And I thought, what the frig am I trying to do? Why don't I just pack it in, stay here and join in the singing? . . . But when I turned around my mother had stopped singing and was crying. I said, "Why are you crying, mother?" and she said "There must be better songs to sing than this." And I thought, "Yeah, that's what I'm trying to do – sing a better song."'

Two iconic 1980s movies: *Educating Rita* (1983) and *Wall Street* (1987). On first viewing both involve central characters that couldn't be further apart. Rita (Julie Walters) is the eponymous heroine of Willy Russell's masterful screenplay, which includes the above quote as the feisty Rita tackles the strains of escaping her fate as a baby-factory for her working-class clan. Gordon Gekko (Michael Douglas), meanwhile, is Wall Street's billionaire corporate raider and detested anti-hero of Oliver Stone's defining homage to a decade of excess. He's a ruthless maverick – a lone wolf reaping havoc among the fat cats of corporate America.

Yet both are outsiders. And both illustrate key characteristics for any outsider searching for meaning through creativity. First, that there's no single path towards redemption: both Rita and Gekko are leveraging their frustrations – Rita fighting the narrow expectations or her cultural poverty, Gekko the cosy elite of Ivy League WASPs that run (and ruin, according to Gekko) the 'malfunctioning organization called the USA'.

Second, both are utilizing their creativity in their search for meaning: Rita via an *Open University* English literature degree tutored by the alcoholic Frank (Michael Caine); Gekko through his (not always legal) financial wizardry and by the wielding of his Machiavellian mastery over stooges such as Bud Fox (Charlie Sheen).

Both also reveal the true aptitude of the outsider with respect to forging an *edge*: overcoming barriers through sheer grit rather than in the miraculous application of genuine disadvantages – as Gladwell would have us believe. Both celebrate the outsider's ability, when motivated, to observe, learn and assume chameleon-like qualities to extract what's needed (often from insiders) for their selfish ends. Sure, Rita assumes some of the pretentions of her acquired university friends, as she should. Yet her external viewpoint remains intact – giving her the strength, for instance, to deal with the addictions and melancholy of those in her new, elevated, circle. Gekko, on the other hand, uses his wealth and power to 'liberate' publicly-listed corporations from the dead hand of stodgy self-serving managers, as his famous 'greed is good' speech attests.

Of course, both are motivated by what they're escaping or barred from. And both exhibit sociopathic tendencies in their determination to achieve their goals (Rita secretly taking contraceptive pills, for instance). Of course, Gekko's behaviour is even psychopathic – resulting ultimately in his arrest for instigating an insider-trading scam.

'If you're not inside you're outside,' he yells at Fox, to justify his illegality, revealing both Gekko's disrespect for insiders – which includes Brits thinking 'they were born with a better pot to piss in' – and his psychopathic determination to enter their lair, if only to destroy it from within.

An unrepentant individualist

Of course, *Wall Street* is a typical Hollywood morality tale – meaning that the narrative requires Gekko's comeuppance. In reality, many Gekko-types develop legally-sustainable and meaningful lives having reached the top of Maslow's hierarchy, albeit ones requiring shallow acquisition to get there. That said, as outsiders – not necessarily 'handicapped' by conscience – we should absorb Hollywood's warning regarding boundaries.

Certainly, Gekko's iconoclastic self-determination makes him a fictional hero for many outsiders – especially those in finance who just as often quote the opening segment of his 'greed is good' speech. Here he lambasts the 33 insiders running *Teldar Paper* – a loss-making company Gekko's in the process of 'liberating' – for 'all the paperwork going back and forth between all these vice presidents' as well as their 'steak lunches, hunting and fishing trips, corporate jets and golden parachutes'.

'The new law of evolution in corporate America seems to be the survival of the unfittest,' he claims – pointing at the self-satisfied insiders all lined up on the podium and fearing this outsider's destructive creativity.

Don't get me wrong: it's not Gekko's unfettered free market capitalism I'm admiring – just as it wasn't the protester's politics I railed against in Chapter 13. I'm as impressed by anti-capitalist outsiders: men such as *Beatles* frontman, cultural revolutionary and original 'working class hero' John Lennon (1940–1980) – born to a wayward Liverpool merchant seaman of Irish descent; Labour Party founder Keir Hardie (1856–1915) – raised by a domestic servant in a one-room Lanarkshire cottage; Nye Bevan (1897–1960) – architect of the National Health Service, though a Welsh coalminer at 13 with a stammer and poor school record; and Jimmy Reid (1932–2010) – the firebrand Clyde shipyard union-leader who innovated the 'work in' (an alternative to striking in which workers occupied the yard while completing orders).

It's Gekko the enemy of insiders I admire. Many cite Gekko's 'greed is good' mantra as the cause of the calamities to befall the financial system in 2008, though Gekko would no doubt cite the managerial greed of insiders – of 'rent-seekers' gambling with other peoples' money – as the cause. Yet, for me – and many outsiders – he's an unrepentant individualist: a man leveraging his own outsider instincts and insecurities to drive him ever higher. To continually sharpen his *edge*.

No tribe or clan, no club or conference

So take your pick. Having found their path, both Rita and Gekko are legitimate role-models for outsiders trying to escape the confines of their narrow predestination. Personally, I seem to fall between the two: not as working class as Rita, though still escaping what I saw as my limiting cultural horizons through adult education; not as rich, powerful, or Machiavellian as Gekko (not even close), though still finding meaning through a convention-breaking brand of entrepreneurialism after detesting the greasy pole of corporate life.

Certainly, I remain an outsider. There's no tribe or clan to which I belong, no clubs of which I'm a member (I was a guest at the *Ivy Club*, in case you wondered). I have no annual conference at which to network and no awards dinner in which to congratulate my peers or lobby for their acclaim. And I pursue no sport or hobbies likely to bring me clubhouse bonhomie. Indeed, I conform exactly to the Groucho rule with respect to clubs – feeling uncomfortable the moment any group assumes I'm 'clubbable' and invites me into *their* temple or to take part in *their* rituals.

But I'm not lost like Holden Caulfield. Nor am I frustrated like Franz Kafka, lonely like Travis Bickle or even cynical like Alvy Singer. At least, not anymore. Like Rita and Gekko, I'm found. My life has meaning, although I also see it as a journey rather than a destination. I've used entrepreneurial creativity to give my life context and expect to add further texture as the years go by –

thanks, in part, to a growth mindset, though one I have to reinforce almost daily.

Now in my late forties, my life finally makes sense – partly because I've spent so much time searching for meaning, including long periods staring out of café windows pondering the agony of it all. Of course, the answer wasn't beyond the window. There was no one 'out there' waiting to hand me meaning, though plenty wanted help with their own quests and were prepared to recruit this lost soul to their cause. As cheesy as it sounds, I found meaning from within.

Ultimately, it was in using all that negativity and frustration – and in leveraging the grit required to overcome the real disadvantages of my educational background – that offered me a way forward. That's what gave me my *edge* – sheer bloody determination, as well as the utilization of my journalistic skills to both write best-selling books and create a successful PR company.

The danger of recruitment

Even once meaning's found, dangers remain for the outsider, however. As stated, recruitment is one. We're vulnerable to radicalism, which can lead us into the arms of people that – despite appearances – do not have our best interests at heart.

Bubbling away while writing this book has been news of radicalized and recruited British Asians being sacrificed – in Syria and Iraq – for the greater cause of Jihad. This is usually as articulated by privileged and well-connected leaders, including Mohammed Al-Arifi, the well-heeled Saudi theologian accused of radicalizing Muslim adolescents while preaching in British mosques. Many of these young Jihadists are outsiders – alienated by racist abuse in their hometowns, as well as the poverty of their outlook. Far from being the most vulnerable, however, many will be the most intelligent of their peers. They'll be well aware of the hurdles young Asians face in cities long since bereft of the industries that enticed their parents (and even grandparents) as economic migrants.

Adventure, adrenalin, belonging – *meaning*: it's a heady brew for young and alienated outsiders stuck in rust-belt conurbations. But it's a lie, told to those seeking *something*. Even death is glamorized, although for me it's a wasted life: a lost – stolen – opportunity. And the best way of avoiding such a theft is by finding your own meaning, not one rendering you as cannon fodder for the grandiose vanities of the well-born.

The curse of being cool

Two other dangers require listing. The first I call the 'curse of being cool' – the idea of hiding behind a serene, detached veneer in order to feign disinterest or even attempt a silent hierarchy over others. The cool give the outward impression of nonchalance, or of being too focused on the aesthetic to worry about or even notice the troubled agitations of others. It's a defence mechanism, of course. Yet it's a pervasive one among the young, not least because it hides a cacophony of inner issues – including pride, fear and a nagging sense of inadequacy. And yes it's a curse, because being cool is a self-imposed emotional impediment – a tyranny and a burden – that inevitably leads nowhere: blunting rather than sharpening our *edge*.

In Chapter 10 I mentioned the iconic image of James Dean in Times Square – hands in pocket, collar up, cigarette in mouth. It's probably the most instantly recognizable image of 'cool' ever captured. Yet it could only ever be a photograph – a snapshot – because Dean can't stay cool forever. He has to move on. Do stuff. And that involves uncool behaviour. Just as my attempt at mimicking Dean was corrupted by meetings, so he'll need to source money, food and accommodation. He'll have to deal with others: compromise – obey rules. And that looks like desperate behaviour for the cool guy, chained as he is to his own self-image of proud mental detachment.

Of course, the alternative is that he carries on kicking around Times Square with nowhere to go. But that instantly turns the world's coolest image into one of its saddest. Suddenly, Dean's reduced to Caulfield – just another out-of-town kid trying to blag his way among the sophisticates of the big city. Far better to decide what you want, settle on a strategy, and then go on a mission to get it: obeying the rules that need obeying and making the compromises required to get there – all in the knowledge that it's *your* mission that counts. Nothing else.

The trap of revenge

And the second thing to guard against is what I call the 'trap of revenge'. Too often we spend time benchmarking our progress in purely negative terms – against something, or more usually someone, that we perceive has harmed us or held us down. This is most often someone in our family, although it can be school or college 'friends', teachers, former or current colleagues, or even 'them' (men, white people, 'the rich', etc.).

Again, such a countenance can be initially enabling – part of the 'screw you' motivation mentioned in Part Two. Yet over the long term it's a highly-disabling trait, and one that prevents you ever escaping your tormentor/s. They're forever in your head, a defining and negative part of you. And that will stall your mental progress – wrecking judgement and blighting creativity – not least because any setback will conjure their taunting image, dragging you right back to when you were at your weakest.

It's also unnecessary, not least because, as English poet George Herbert (1593–1633) wrote, 'living well is the best revenge'. That's not a call to acquire a wonderful life and then throw it in their face, potentially after seeking them out for this purpose. Such emotional immaturity will compound the obsession as well as make you look and feel a fool. It may also backfire, perhaps with them throwing *their* achievements back at you.

Instead it's a call for insight. For developing your own yardstick based on having found, or still finding, meaning. And then focusing on that – rather than the mentally-harmful imprisonment of anger, revenge, or even final victory over a rival. In fact, real – sustainable – victory comes from embracing your 'enemies': synergizing with them, perhaps exploring win-win opportunities. It also comes from understanding *their* agonies, which will be every bit as great as your own, although may require a viewpoint-shift to notice. It certainly doesn't come from 'vanquishing' them, as even psychopaths such as Gekko learnt in the end.

An extraordinary vantage point

I began with Malcolm Gladwell's book *David and Goliath* and that's where I'll end. It's a myth, I stated, to claim that being a 'misfit' or outsider is advantageous when, in fact, it's an outlook full of disabling disadvantages, not least the mental impairment (however acquired) that put us on the edge in the first place. Yet he's right in one respect: being a genuine, disadvantaged, outsider offers us extraordinary perspective – something Viktor Frankl noticed even while incarcerated in the most appalling circumstances.

Being on the outside looking in is not always a comforting view. But it's the view we have nonetheless. And since we're here anyway we may as well profit from that extraordinary vantage point, not least because – the moment we're on the inside – we'll immediately start looking for the exit.

Outsiders have an extraordinary vantage point. Yet, until we learn to convert that skewed view into something positive – with meaning – as well as something both offering and generating an edge, it's one that will remain genuinely disabling. Find meaning, however, and the door is opened to becoming an unrepentant outsider: the rebel with a cause. And that's certainly a goal worth striving for.

---

10 RULES FOR OUTSIDERS TO OBEY

Asking outsiders to obey rules is like asking dogs to share a bone or cats to be kind to mice: it goes against our nature. Yet – with those mental limitations very much in mind – the following should help outsiders forge their *edge* within a world where insiders, unfortunately, make most of the rules.

1. *Understand and accept who you are.* There's no point wanting to be somebody else, not least because it's impossible. Instead, develop insight. Understand the early-life conditioning that made you who you are, not least because it's cathartic and should help you accept yourself. That said, self-criticism can be motivational, so accepting who you are is not a call for self-satisfaction – within limits, frustration can be a strong driver.

2. *Find your meaning.* Deciding your life is pointless is a self-fulfilling prophesy. So reject such defeatism in favour of a more enabling outlook: one that gives your life meaning. Your discomfort with your surroundings is simply the negative part of that discovery – telling you to get looking. Yet meaning won't come in a flash of light – it evolves from following the right paths, often from developing your *edge* in some shape or form. None-theless, have faith: there's a sustainable niche for you to call your own, though it'll only be your niche if you make it yourself.

3. *Adopt a growth mindset.* Unfortunately, many outsiders have a fixed mindset, which generates barriers for your progress by assuming your attributes are set in stone. To find meaning, you

must open your mind to growth – assuming every encounter is a chance to learn more. Of course, it's easy to flip into a growth mindset. But it's even easier to lapse back into a fixed one. So remind yourself daily that growth is important.

4. *Nurture your insight.* It's a myth that outsiders possess ingrained advantages. But they do have disadvantages they can use to motivate themselves. Poor educational attainment is just one example – meaning we value more the education we pursue in adulthood. Poverty is another, meaning we'll understand the value of money. Even physical disabilities fall into this category – as any Paralympian athlete can tell you. That said, outsiders do have one advantage: a unique vantage point, allowing them insight as the observer of others. This offers them an *edge*, but also makes them highly creative (in whatever form): something they should nurture.

5. *Participate.* Outsiders can assume the world's a horrible place full of phony people affecting false sincerity – as Holden Caulfield will tell you. Yet our response shouldn't be a refusal to participate, which will foster failure, loneliness and despair. Instead, we should participate. Of course, it's vital we find the right *thing* in which to participate – hence the (sometimes agonizing) search for meaning. And – within reason – we should only participate on our own terms (although some compromise is inevitable).

6. *Develop good judgement.* The insight we develop as an outsider will be wasted unless we become strong decision-makers. Too often, good judgement is viewed as the removal of emotions from our decision-making, when – in reality – it's impossible to divorce the two. So we should accept emotion's role while ensuring it remains just one aspect. In fact, the strongest judgement comes from pursuing well-articulated goals via a thought-through strategy.

7. *Beware pride.* There are many disabling traits outsiders need to overcome: anger, negativity, cynicism, defeatism, extremism and misdirected sociopathy among them. Yet many come down

to pride – an overblown concern regarding dignity that can prevent actions being taken for fear of humiliation. The 'curse of being cool' forms part of this, which is a near-paralyzing trait because progress requires us to do uncool things that may prove humiliating.

8. *Accept that they'll always be a boss.* Many outsiders become entrepreneurs in order to avoid working for others. Quite right too. Yet that won't kill the need to please other people. Gatekeepers – those that have what we need in their gift – are inevitable. Hopefully, no single person will be critical, but some humility will be a strategic requirement for outsiders trying to find meaning.

9. *Serve your apprenticeship.* Genius is a myth – even Mozart was trained by his father from a very young age. So there's a price to be paid for forging that all-important *edge*. Artists, writers, designers, even entrepreneurs: all need to serve an apprentice-ship that hones their craft or skill. Of course, the idea of 'serving your apprenticeship' fits well with both a growth mindset and the avoidance of pride as a barrier to achievement. Yet it's something outsiders can detest. So why not see life *always* as an apprenticeship for the next level? It will revolutionize your outlook.

10. *Value your progress.* Finally, we should remember that the journey's the thing, not the destination. That way, we'll value the advances we make knowing that – while better's to come – our current position is also worth celebrating. Too often, outsiders are so busy fighting the demons within they fail to value their progress. Partly, this is healthy: we must guard against complacency. Yet failing to acknowledge our progress makes us vulnerable to catastrophizing the smallest setback, which can immediately blunt the *edge* we've just spent years sharpening. In fact, there's no harm in marking our progress with a quiet sense of self-satisfaction, as long as we accept that – come tomorrow – the battle starts all over again.

BIBLIOGRAPHY

Agness, Lindsey (2008) *Change Your Life with NLP*, Harlow, UK: Pearson Education.

Arden, Paul (2003) *It's Not How Good You Are, It's How Good You Want to Be*, London: Phaidon Press.

Argyle, Michael (1967) *The Psychology of Interpersonal Behaviour*, London: Penguin Books.

Bayley, Stephen and Mavity, Roger (2007) *Life's a Pitch*, London: Bantam Press.

Boeree, C. George (2002) *A Bio-Social Theory of Neurosis*, Shippensburg, PA: Shippensburg University.

Bronson, Po (2003) *What Should I Do With My Life?* New York: Random House.

Burstein, Julie (2011) *Spark: How Creativity Works*, London: Harper Paperbacks.

Camus, Albert (1942) (2007 translation) *The Myth of Sisyphus*, London: Great Penguin Ideas.

Camus, Albert (1942) (2013 translation) *The Outsider (L'Etranger)*, Paris: Librairie Gallimard/London: Penguin Modern Classics.

Clance, Pauline and Imes, Suzanne (1978) *The Imposter Phenomenon Among High Achieving Women*, Atlanta, GA: Georgia State University (academic paper).

Covey, Stephen (1989) *The Seven Habits of Highly Effective People*, London: Simon & Schuster.

Crumb, Robert and Zane Mairowitz, David (2007) *Kafka*, Seattle, WA: Fantagraphics Books.

de Bono, Edward (1985) *Six Thinking Hats*, New York: Little Brown.

de Botton, Alain (2005) *Status Anxiety*, London: Penguin Books.

Dennis, Felix (2006) *How to Get Rich*, London: Ebury Press.

Diamond, Stephen A. (1999) *Anger, Madness, and the Daimonic: The Psychological Genesis of Violence, Evil and Creativity* New York: State University of New York Press.

Dutton, Kevin and McNab, Andy (2014) *The Good Psychopath's Guide to Success*, London: Bantam Press.

Dweck, Carol (2006) *Mindset: The New Psychology of Success*, New York: Ballantine Books.

Ellis, Albert (2009) *All Out!: An Autobiography*, Amherst, NY: Prometheus Books.

Erikson, Erik (1968) *Identity: Youth and Crisis*, New York: W.M. Norton & Company.

Fennell, Melanie (1999) *Overcoming Low Self-Esteem*, London: Constable & Robinson.

Foley, Michael (2010) *The Age of Absurdity*, London: Simon & Schuster.

Fox, Nik Farrel (2006) *The New Sartre*, London: The Continuum International Publishing Group.

Frankl, Viktor (1949) (2004 translation) *Man's Search for Meaning*, London: Ebury Publishing/London: Rider.

Fraser, Antonia (1996) *The Gunpowder Plot*, London: Mandarin Paperbooks.

Gain, Laurence (2013) *Introducing Nietzsche*, London: Icon Books.

Gladwell, Malcolm (2013) *David and Goliath: Underdogs, Misfits and the Art of Battling Giants*, London: Penguin Books.

Goleman, David (1996) *Emotional Intelligence*, London: Bloomsbury.

Gross, Richard (2005) *Psychology: The Science of Mind and Behaviour*, Abingdon, UK: Hodder Arnold.

Gross, Richard and Kinnison, Nancy (2007) *Psychology for Nurses*, Abingdon, UK: Hodder Arnold.

Heath, Chip and Dan (2013) *Decisive: How to Make Better Decisions*, New York: Crown Business.

Hitchins, Christopher (2003) *Why Orwell Matters*, London: Basic Books.

Holiday, Ryan (2014) *The Obstacle is The Way: The Ancient Art of Turning Adversity to Advantage*, London: Profile Books.

Isaacson, Walter (2011) *Steve Jobs*, London: Little Brown.

Isenberg, Daniel (2013) *Worthless, Impossible and Stupid*, Boston, MA: Harvard Business Review.

James, Oliver (2002) *They F*** You Up*, London: Bloomsbury.

Johnson, Luke (2007) *The Maverick*, Petersfield, UK: Harriman House.

Johnson, Luke (2011) *Start It Up*, London: Portfolio Penguin.

Kafka, Franz (2014) *The Essential Kafka: The Castle; The Trial; Metamorphosis and Other Stories*, London: Wordsworth Classics.

Keller, Jeff (2012) *Attitude is Everything*, New Delhi: Pentagon Press.

Kierkegaard, Søren (1844) (1980 translation) *The Concept of Anxiety*, Princeton, NJ; Princeton University Press.

Klein, Gary (2014) *Seeing What Others Don't*, Boston, MA: Nicholas Brealey Publishing.

Krznaric, Roman (2012) *How to Find Fulfilling Work*, London: Macmillan.

Land, George and Jarman, Beth (1998) *Breakpoint and Beyond: Mastering the Future*, Carlsbad, CA: Leadership 2000 Inc.

Marcia, James (1980) *Identity in Adolescence* (in *The Handbook of Adolescent Psychology*: ed. Adelson, J.), Hoboken, NJ: John Wiley & Sons.

Mariowitz, David (2012) *Introducing Camus*, London: Icon Books.

Maslow, Abraham (1943) *A Theory of Human Motivation*, Washington, DC: *Psychological Review* 50(4), 370–396.

McGowan, Bill (2014) *Pitch Perfect*, London: HarperBusiness.

Mitchell, Sally (1996) *Daily Life in Victorian England*, London: Greenwood.

Morris, Desmond (1967) *The Naked Ape*, London: Jonathan Cape.

Nietzsche, Friedrich (1878) (1994 translation) *Human, All Too Human*, London: Penguin Classics.

Nietzsche, Friedrich (1885) (1974 translation) *Thus Spoke Zarathustra*, London: Penguin Classics.

Norem, Julie (2002) *The Positive Power of Negative Thinking*, New York: Basic Books.

Oliver, Charles M. (1999) *Ernest Hemingway A to Z*, New York: Checkmark Books.

Orwell, George (1933) *Down and Out in Paris and London*, London: Victor Gollancz.

Orwell, George (1945) *Animal Farm*, London: Victor Gollancz.

Perry, Grayson and Jones, Wendy (2007) *Portrait of the Artist as a Young Girl*, London: Vintage.

Pink, Daniel H. (2012) *To Sell is Human*, New York: Riverhead Books.

Pinkard, Terry P. (2000) *Hegel: A Biography*, Cambridge: Cambridge University Press.

Robinson, Ken (2001) *Out of Our Minds: Learning to be Creative*, Chichester, UK: Capstone.

Robinson, Ken (2014) *Finding Your Element*, London: Penguin Books.

Ronson, Jon, (2011) *The Psychopath Test*, London: Picador.

Rousseau, Jean-Jacques (1754) (2014 translation) *Discourse on the Origin and Basis of Inequality Among Men*, Holland: Marc-Michel Ray/Seattle WA: CreateSpace Independent Publishing Platform.

Rumelt, Richard (2011) *Good Strategy, Bad Strategy*, New York: Crown Business.

Salinger, J.D. (1951) *The Catcher in the Rye*, Boston, MA: Little Brown.

Sartre, Jean-Paul (1938) (2000 translation) *Nausea*, London: Penguin Modern Classics.

Sartre, Jean-Paul (1946) (2007 translation) *Existentialism is a Humanism*, New Haven, CT: Yale University Press.

Sheldon, Michael (1991) *Orwell: The Authorised Biography*, London: William Heinemann Ltd.

Silet, Charles L.P. (ed.) (2006) *The Films of Woody Allen: Critical Essays*, Lanham, MD: Scarecrow Press.

Simmons, Roberta G., Blyth, Dale A. (1987) *Moving into Adolescence: The Impact of Pubertal Change and School Context*, New York: A. de Gruyter.

Sinclair, Iain (2002) *London Orbital*, London: Penguin Books.

Smith, J.A. (translator) (2006) *On the Soul, Aristotle*, New York: Digireads. com.

Solomon, Robert C. (1974) *Existentialism*, New York: McGraw Hill.

Stout, Martha (2005) *The Sociopath Next Door*, New York: Broadway Books.

Sweet, Corinne (2010) *Change Your Life with CBT*, Harlow, UK: Prentice Hall Life.

Swenson, David F. (2000) *Something About Kierkegaard*, Macon, GA: Mercer University Press.

Thoby, Philip and Read, Howard (2011) *Introducing Sartre*, London: Icon Books.

Wallas, Graham (1926) *The Art of Thought*, Nottingham: All Answers Ltd.

Wilson, Colin (1956) *The Outsider*, London: Victor Gollancz.

Wood, Michael (2006) *In Search of the Dark Ages*, London: BBC Books.

Woodfin, Rupert and Groves, Judy (2013) *Introducing Aristotle*, London: Icon Books.

Yeung, Dr Rob (2014) *How to Win*, Chichester, UK: Capstone.

Young, Hugo (1989) *One of Us*, London: MacMillan.

Young, James Webb (1965) *A Technique for Producing Ideas*, New York: McGraw-Hill.

ABOUT ROBERT KELSEY

Photo credit:
Matthew Plummer

Robert Kelsey is a best-selling author, occasional speaker, and the owner and CEO of a successful financial PR agency in the City of London. His series of books on the insecurities that made him such an ineffective young adult have sold over 100,000 copies and have been translated into 10 languages. Yet Robert has always felt like an outsider. This is largely due to the tribal dislocation of his childhood – his parents being part of the post-war East London Diaspora to rural Essex: 'townies marooned in the countryside' as he describes it. But it was also due to a low self-esteem generated from family strains as well as the biological constraints of his late onset adolescence.

Yet, once ingrained, the notion of being an outsider has never left him. Whether as the sensitive youngster in the macho world of the building industry; the 'mature' student among the teenage under-graduates at university; the state-educated rough-diamond among the privately-educated sophisticates of the publishing industry; or the deep-thinker among the deal-junkies of investment banking, Robert has always been a fish out of water.

And far from an enabling outlook – as many commentators on the phenomenon of outsidership love to preach – such a skewed view-point has been incredibly disabling. Sensitivity, paranoia, reactivity and anger have been constant companions during Robert's some-times quixotic quests: often generating self-fulfilling behaviours that have, indeed, confirmed his outsider status.

Even as a mature adult having returned to his tribal ancestral 'homelands' (Hackney, to be precise), Robert is the one among the many. Alone in the crowd, he's irritated by hipsters opening clubs he cannot join, yet is also abused for being a middle-class interloper, polluting this rejectionists' bohemian enclave.

The Outside Edge is Robert's fifth book, and the fourth in his series exploring his own failings. His view is that 'smart people' can be disabled by their insecurities, far more than many realize. Yet they also have it within them to overcome such barriers and make progress anyway – having understood the issues and accepted who they are. While being 'cured' is, in his view, a false promise made to desperate people, understanding and acceptance are the first steps to generating objectives, plans and strategies that take both the sufferer, and their mental baggage, to a better place.

Robert's aim is not to turn the outsider into an insider – a solution that's probably impossible anyway (with much blood, sweat and tears expended in the effort). Instead, he intends to help people lose the disablement of being an outsider by generating their own path – one that both offers meaning and helps forge their unique *edge*. After all – having exhausted all the alternatives – that's exactly what he did.

INDEX

Index